DIRECT CONNECTION

Transformation of Consciousness

DIRECT CONNECTION
Transformation of Consciousness

Judith S. Miller, Ph.D.

Rutledge Books, Inc. Danbury, CT

No portions of this text may be reproduced, stored in a retrieval system, or transmitted in any form or by any means, electronic or mechanical, including photocopy, without prior consent of Judith S. Miller.

Copyright © 2000 by Judith S. Miller
All rights reserved under the International and Pan-American Copyright Conventions.

ALL RIGHTS RESERVED
Rutledge Books, Inc.
107 Mill Plain Road, Danbury, CT 06811
1-800-278-8533
www.rutledgebooks.com

Manufactured in the United States of America

Cataloging in Publication Data
Miller, Judith S.
   Direct Connection: Transformation of Consciousness

ISBN: 1-58244-077-8

  1. Spiritual healing. 2. Psychology and religion.
3. Psychotherapy -- Religious aspects.

Library of Congress Catalog Number: 99-069142

"This is what psychotherapy at the brink of a new millennium needs: an engaged and radical reflection on the relationship between psychology and spirituality. Dr. Judith Miller integrates within her book the story of her own psycho-spiritual opening and the transformative potential arising out of her psychotherapeutic work with others. This book is an important contribution to the fields of mental health and consciousness research. It is a gift with the potential to engage peace and joy within the global mind."

— Ingo Jahrsetz, Ph.D., Director of the School of Transpersonal Psychology and Psychotherapy, Freiberg, Germany, and author of *Holotropic Breathwork—Psychotherapy and Spiritually*

"Dr. Judith Miller displays exceptional courage and vision as a traditionally trained clinical psychologist, in sharing this evocative and thought provoking story of the spiritually transformative experiences which have highlighted her and her clients' lives. This open sharing of her personal journey along the Mystical Path is an inspiration to readers and challenges them to expand their own view of reality to include the possibility of every person's potential for experiences of direct connection to the Higher Power. Well done!"

— Yvonne Kason, MD., author of *A Farther Shore: How Near-Death and other Extraordinary Experiences can change Ordinary Lives.*

"Dr. Judith Miller's book has a great significance in our times of shifting consciousness, showing us our responsibility to offer guidance to those who suffer spiritual crises and are marginalized by mainstream psychology as mentally ill. Sharing her own mystical experiences, her message is very clear. What we call the Unknown is our Common Ground."

— Tanna Jakubowicz-Mount, President of the Polish Transpersonal Association, Vice President of the European Transpersonal Association, Warsaw, Poland.

Contents

Acknowledgements (ix)

Author's Note (xi)

Preface (xiii)

Introduction (xv)

PART I *TODAY, YESTERDAY, AND TOMORROW (1)*

1. A New Way of Working

2. In the Beginning

3. The Art of Dying

PART II *A FOOT IN TWO WORLDS (59)*

4. A Priest and the Tree of Life

5. Shamanism and Spiritual Initiation

6. Beyond Time and Space

PART III *OUR TRUE NATURE (107)*

7. Identity Crisis: Christian Mysticism

8. Process That Never Ends

9. Unitive Experience

PART IV TRANSFORMATION: OVERCOMING POLARITIES (145)

10. The Divine Feminine

11. Healing at Auschwitz: The Wall Came Down

12. Good and Evil

13. Garden of the Soul

14. Transformation of Consciousness

CHAPTER NOTES (215)

ABOUT THE AUTHOR (243)

Acknowledgements

This book is dedicated Martin Miller, my husband and best friend. Your unconditional love and acceptance has brought joy to my life, and has enabled me to keep moving forward and not to look back;

I am appreciative to my children, Philip and Marjorie Miller, who deeply care about me, authentically engage with me, teach me a great deal, and are always there—each in your unique ways;

I also acknowledge the following people:

Lisa Miller and Jonathon Shapiro who bring much happiness and light to our whole family;

The courageous people who have trusted me as they travel life paths;

Stanislav Grof, an important teacher of mine;

The late Peter Dorman, whose understanding, editorial skills, attention to detail and open heart have greatly contributed to the birth of *Direct Connection*;

Thanks also to those people whose support at different times was important in the development of this book: Tony Parrotto, Maura Curran, Irv Rutman, Dianne Seaman, and John Amorsa; and the

Rutledge Group: Art Salzfass, Marilyn Smith, John Laub, Joy O'Brien and Kristin Winstanley;

Finally, gratitude to my mother, the late Dorothy Gordon Kort, for bringing me into this world, and to my father, Henry Sklar, and brother, Nathan Sklar, who have been encouraging of me and my work over the years.

Author's Note

The case histories and personal stories included in this book are based on actual experiences. In order to protect the confidentiality and anonymity of the individuals involved, I have paraphrased their stories and have modified some small details and identifying features. For those people who agreed to have their identities known, their accounts remain in their own words and their names are given.

Appreciation is extended to all of them for the courage and commitment they have demonstrated to their own growth and development and for their contribution in assisting the collective to reach the next phase in its evolution.

Preface

In this book, I describe another way to understand reality, a reality that goes far beyond what I was taught during my university training to become a psychologist. I discuss a radical way of understanding human nature that is not accepted by societal institutions-specifically, academia, psychiatry, medicine, and organized religion. I describe how I was led to this new revelation through my personal story and the stories of people I have worked with as well. This book documents the often unbelievable ways that information regarding our human nature has come to me and those people with whom I work. It is understandable that some readers may be skeptical at first.

Our stories exemplify what I call the direct connection. This phenomenon has been identified by others in different ways. Psychiatrists call it psychotic thinking. Shamans and other indigenous healers understand it as magic and consider it to be sacred. Prophets and mystics refer to it as spiritual consciousness. The mythologist Joseph Campbell describes it as the "Hero's Journey."

The purpose of this book is to illustrate how the direct connection is available to all individuals and how it reflects our true mystical nature. Being in touch with one's mystical nature means connecting with an ultimate wisdom that is outside of time and space and is filled with true information that does not seem to be coming from one's subjective awareness. "All mystics," said Saint Martin, "speak the same language. The place which they happen to occupy in the kingdom of this world matters little."

Most people in my small corner of the world identify me as a contemporary woman, a psychologist and college professor, married with two young adult children. Before I became aware of my direct connection, I fluctuated between considering myself an agnostic and regarding myself as an atheist. Now, I know that the path on which I have been catapulted, through no intention of my own, is one that all people can access.

Direct Connection: A Transformation of Consciousness is more than my story and my clients' stories; it is a universal story for our time. Not only does this narrative illustrate how human nature can be greatly expanded, but it challenges the existing definitions of mental illness and mental health. We must all begin to acknowledge the existence of an ultimate intelligence that goes beyond our own. To access, integrate, and act upon the meaning of this intelligence will empower us each to transform ourselves and our world.

Introduction

I am not a celebrity. My name is not well-known in the halls of academia or in religious circles. However, I do have important information to share-information that has been voiced for thousands of years, but that is not acknowledged by experts or by institutions of our society.

Professionally, I no longer identify only with the field of psychology. Although I hold a doctoral degree in psychology, my primary identity at this time, the one I nourish most deeply within myself, is that of a person who has made a direct connection with a reality larger than our physical world. As a mystic, my direct connection with a higher force has come to signify the truth. The information that I have to share with you is deeply embedded within every human being. Some people have access to it, and for others it is covered up. Societal dogma has cut most people off from their true inner nature.

Virtually all spiritual traditions have claimed that mystical insight pertaining to Buddha nature, Christ consciousness, the Tao, or Brahman is a reality that exists independently of other experience. These traditions have also held that this reality is objective and can be understood through spiritual practices that result in certain direct experiences. These experiences have been confirmed by mystics cross-culturally throughout history. Thus, great thinkers since antiquity have given the claims of mystical knowledge a central place in their own philosophies. Since an abundance of evidence corroborates mystical knowledge, any exclusion of these accounts of human nature represents extreme tunnel vision. Here, a statement made by Albert Einstein is applicable:

> The most beautiful and most profound emotion we can experience is the sensation of the mystical. It is the sower of all true science. He to whom this emotion is a stranger, who can no longer wonder and stand rapt in awe, is as good as dead. To know that what is impenetrable to us really exists, manifesting itself as the highest wisdom and the most radiant beauty which our dull faculties can comprehend only in their most primitive forms-this knowledge, this feeling is at the center of true religiousness. (Lincoln Barnett, *The Universe and Dr. Einstein*, p. 108)

It is time for our culture to wake up and acknowledge the truth. Organized religions need to expand their thinking and help people make the direct connection. Psychiatry must recognize that human nature far exceeds the physiological processes of brain chemistry. Stigmatizing psychiatric diagnoses and numbing psychotropic medications have dulled the spirit of millions of people for far too long.

The knowledge that I have received on my developmental journey has come to me directly and symbolically through visions and dreams, through books and places in the world to which I have been guided, by deep meditative experiences, by teachers who have come into my life in the form of men, women, children, and animals, and by miracles that have transcended three-dimensional time and space. In the following paragraphs I identify ten universal concepts that I have learned not from school or religion, but from the experiences I describe in the book. As you begin to think about these ten concepts, I ask you to answer the questions that are posed in connection with them. These questions will help you to start thinking about the ways that this information is relevant to your everyday life. Through this process, I am hopeful that you will slowly begin to uncover the deepest part of yourself-that part whereby you, too, can make the direct connection.

1. There is an order and purpose for each of our lives.
How many times have you looked back at significant and sometimes difficult events or people who came into your life and then later recognized an important reason why these things happened, that somehow these events or people led you to a place where you could more easily realize your potential?

2. Essential reality provides the opportunity to see the past, present, and future at any given moment in time.
Remember the time that you knew a particular person would call you, and then he did? What about the time you had a premonition that a loved one would have a problem? How did you explain this to yourself when your "hunch" turned out to be true?

3. Beyond the five senses, there is no separation between mind and matter.
Have you ever had a thought that you saw materialize in the world? For example, a woman wonders if she should call her estranged lover. She turns on the radio and hears the song "Call Him Now." She dials his number, they reconcile and live happily ever after. How many times have such "coincidences" made you

feel either that you were going crazy or that "magic" had replaced the rational world?

4. The core self or soul survives forever. After a long process of development-incorporating many lives-it will eventually perfect itself.
Have you ever visited a place, met a person, or felt an allegiance or identification with a time period or ideology that made you feel that you had known it before, even though in your present lifetime you never had?

5. Sometimes a soul may exist in another realm in spirit form.
How many times have you felt that a deceased loved one was with you in some manner? Usually this feeling is dismissed as a figment of your imagination. People avoid discussing it with others for fear of appearing unstable.

6. In addition to an ultimate force, there are many levels of energy, many realms and dimensions beyond the earth plane.
How have you reacted to the adult or child who says she talks to her guardian angel or to her imaginary friend? What of the stories you have heard about persons who saw a UFO or even had contact with an extraterrestrial? Did you consider such persons silly, uninformed, perhaps crazy?

7. Energy from higher realms can heal.
How have you made sense of the situation in which someone who was diagnosed by a medical specialist as terminally ill survived that illness and became well? Just an unexplained event?

8. An energy force can attach to our fears until these fears are acknowledged and released.
Have you ever intuitively felt that something was wrong in your involvement with a particular person or situation? You can later look back on that experience and question why you stayed in this interaction while having felt such negative energy. You may have been hurt because of the experience, but in retrospect, do you feel that it allowed you to grow?

9. Our true nature is to progress to wholeness and transformation through accessing the direct connection to an expanded reality.
How do you explain a miracle happening in your life? If your initial response is that you have never experienced one, I ask that you think again. You probably repressed recognition of it as a miracle, because you didn't know how to conceptualize it. We have all experienced miracles, events that go beyond time and space, maybe a feeling of connection to something so much larger than we understand. Close your eyes, think about this question, and I'm sure you will recall a time when you understood your true nature to be something more than a body and five senses.

10. Beyond time and space, we are one with the ultimate wisdom.
Have you ever found yourself in the presence of someone who seemed more emotionally and spiritually developed than most other people? Have you asked yourself why this was the case, especially if you knew that this person did not grow up in a manner that seemed extraordinary in any way? This person most likely would be in one of the last phases in his or her psychospiritual journey.

Direct Connection discusses a new way for people to travel on a spiritual and psychological path toward higher development.

Future healers—whether they be doctors, clergy, psychologists, or other care givers—must assist people to evolve on their own unique psychospiritual paths. They will help others to understand their own experiences of expanded consciousness; they will help them to integrate the light as well as identify the darkness that enters their lives.

In order for this to occur, a radical shift is needed in our perception of reality. The field of psychiatry must stop defining what is real and not real in the experiences of individuals. Organized religions must open to the possibility that all people have the potential to make direct contact with the ultimate wisdom. The activity of middlemen in the form of doctors or clergy is no longer the correct way. We must accept the fact that each person has his or her unique path and is able to make a direct connection with an ultimate wisdom that our culture identifies as God.

Please come with me now on a remarkable journey. I am hopeful that my own surprising transformation of consciousness will "spark your soul" as we travel together. The spiritual path is the only path that has always existed—and it will continue throughout eternity. Each of you has the capacity to make your own direct connection. When you do, you will join the increasing number of people who are becoming part of a new way of life, a life where you can live in the world in an ordinary manner, and at the same time have experiences that go beyond anything you may have previously imagined.

PART I
Today, Yesterday, and Tomorrow

Our true nature is to progress to wholeness and transformation through accessing the direct connection to an expanded reality.

CHAPTER 1
A New Way of Working

Traveling along an authentic spiritual path is, I believe, the way toward planetary survival. Such a path is what I describe in this book. It is the route that we all are inherently able to embark upon. You may not believe this; you may feel instead that such a path is for a select few. You may see only the weeds that cover the path and not have the confidence or trust to realize that these weeds can be swept away. But the spiritual path can be made clear. I believe that through my story and my clients' stories, you will begin to recognize your own unique paths.

By applying what I've learned through my own direct connection, I am able to assist the people I work with to transform themselves beyond what our culture currently deems possible. The superficiality espoused in religious dogma and behavioral psychology no longer is acceptable. Religion and psychology must come together at their deepest and most authentic points to enable the continual growth of human consciousness.

Why is it that in our society very few people identify with their mystical natures? First, the scientific method has become our God. Society's experts convince themselves and their constituents that any condition that does not fit into their formulas or theorems does not exist. Second, in our society, people who access this reality are often identified as psychotic or mentally ill. This book describes what mental illness is *not* about. As a clinical psychologist, I challenge the conventional definitions of "adjustment" and "good mental health."

Today, there are millions of people who hide the deepest and most profound part of themselves. Mainstream psychiatry, religion, and academia tell them that this core part of their nature is not real, that it is crazy. I believe that these experts have led people astray. Yet, in spite of societal limits, I foresee the time when spiritual consciousness will be more the norm than the exception. People cannot continue to be submerged by authority figures who pathologize their human potential.

WORKING WITH CLIENTS

Overall, there are three major components of my work. First, I assist people to expand their consciousness. This is accomplished through some combination of dream work and meditation. The meditation that my clients engage in occurs in small groups called breath workshops; this approach will be described in detail in later chapters. As they engage in this deep exploration, they begin to have spiritual experiences. These experiences—similar to my experiences described in this book—enable these individuals to contact their core selves, what the mystics call the *sacred ground of the soul*. As they make this contact, they touch the transcendental realm, a realm that lies beyond the limited world of matter and that is merged within the depths of their being.

The second major component of this work is to help people focus on the meaning of these profound occurrences. During individual sessions, we interpret their spiritual experiences together, and then I assist in the process of integration. Most people have spontaneously made contact with these realms at one time or another during their lifetimes. Unfortunately, there is usually no one to help them acknowledge that these experiences are authentic and represent a direct connection to the ultimate wisdom. The mystical experiences of the people I work with are not pushed away out of fear or lack of understanding. This work, by necessity, entails a major shift in their belief system and world view.

The third component is the working through of unresolved emotional problems. As these individuals begin to travel their respective paths, their lives radically change—such that they will never again be what they had been. The psychological or emotional barriers (or both) that had been unresolved are now confronted and worked through. The spiritual energy coming through them forces their conflicted issues to the surface of their consciousness.

My clients fall into three major groups. While retelling some of their stories, I have changed their names and specific biographical details to protect and respect their confidentiality. The first group comprises highly functioning individuals. Many of them are well-educated and hold leadership positions in their professions. While some work in human services, others are business people, lawyers, college professors, physicians, and religious professionals. The men and women in the second group are young adults who often find themselves questioning the values and dictates adhered to by their society. Finally, the third group includes people who have histories of psychiatric diagnoses. Some in this group have progressed to successful functioning; others begin our work together living marginally or primarily unproductive lives.

Despite the differences found among these groups, the work that I do with all of them is essentially the same. A common denominator that they all share is courage. They face and wrestle with their deepest fears and are motivated to live lives of truth and integrity. Typically, I work with them over a two- to three-year period, usually bimonthly, but this can vary. Our work decidedly does not fit into the prevailing model of short-term, problem-focused psychotherapy. It is about soul development and settles for nothing less.

The stories of Heather and Stuart provide a brief overview of the ways in which I work with my clients. These cases demonstrate how direct spiritual experience can have a major influence on any kind of psychological problem. The subjects of these discussions are extremely different from one another in age, gender, life style, and family background.

Heather: Protective Light

Heather is a lovely, blond, blue-eyed woman in her mid-twenties, with a master's degree in social work. She came to me for therapy because of a very traumatic event that had happened to her. After babysitting for the children of a professional couple for over a year, she was attacked and raped by the husband one day when they were alone in his home. She brought him to trial and, as a result, he went to jail. And as if this weren't trauma enough, shortly after we started working together Heather was assaulted by a client in the partial hospitalization unit where she worked. She was also attacked by a coworker.

It would not be surprising if you were to think that this woman might be engaging in some form of unconscious self-destructive behavior that caused these events to occur. However, this was not so.

In our course of working together, it became clear that Heather came from a dysfunctional family system where she had been treated in a humiliating and patronizing manner by her parents and siblings. In spite of her beauty, intelligence, and kindness—or perhaps because of these attributes—she had become the Cinderella of the family. Heather became accustomed to this abusive treatment, since she had experienced it most of her life. As a result, she had difficulty recognizing that there was anything wrong with it. For her, this abuse was a natural condition. It became clear to me early in our work together that Heather was unknowingly participating in a deep process. Though unable to acknowledge emotionally the destructive behavior coming toward her from her family, she was shocked and traumatized by the continuing assaults she experienced from men in the outside world.

During her dreams as well as her meditation (experienced in the breath workshops) she had intense experiences of light and mystical vision. She began to see what appeared to her as the hand of God: this hand reached down to protect her, opened her heart, and let her feel love for the first time in her life. She also began to see a sparking blue eye every time she felt afraid. And through this eye she also felt protection and love. Very soon she began to realize that the spiritual light coming through her was to give her strength. This strength could enable her to deal with the violence that came to her through these men who were attacking her. It also caused her to pay attention to the abuse being directed at her by her family.

Through continued work, Heather was finally able to see her parents for who they were, and she could then confront them and set limits and boundaries for herself. As she was able to do this, her self-concept grew stronger, her relations with her family improved as they began to respect her more, and she became a stronger, happier, more effective person. The darkness that had manifested itself through these attacks dissipated. She found a better job, a successful love relationship, and a firm conviction that her direct connection was there to assure her she would always be protected.

Like Heather, many people have felt intrinsically supported during times of great difficulty. Guidance can come through intuition, dreams, and personal insight.

Stuart: Fighting the Devil

I learned much about the potential of psychospiritual work from Stuart, a handsome, bright-eyed seven-year-old boy. While I had worked with children in the past, it had usually been in a more traditional context. I had never before dealt with children's spiritual experiences as directly as in this case. Stuart's mother contacted me after reading an article in a local newspaper that discussed the spiritual and psychological blending of my work. She described Stuart as someone who had behavioral difficulty at home and at school. He was the only child of two middle class parents, and his mother could not understand why Stuart expressed so much anger towards his parents and schoolmates. She also discussed how he had frequent dreams and nightmares that were very frightening to him.

Upon meeting Stuart for the first time, I was impressed with his intelligence and intuitiveness. He came across as someone much older and wiser than his years would suggest. Our work together was relatively brief. I met with Stuart and his mother for six extended sessions. During this time I asked Stuart to tell me about his dreams, and I learned of the family dynamics between the young boy and each of his parents. The family issues that became apparent were not all that unusual. Briefly, it appeared that Stuart was very close with his mom and more distant from his dad. The roots of this dichotomy derived from a situation that occurred when Stuart was two years old, a time when his father had to work on the West Coast for a year, and Stuart and his mother lived together alone. The subsequent reunion felt harsh for all involved and led to feelings of triangulation that still seemed to be playing out.

Stuart's dream life was more unusual. Although the family was not religious in any way, and did not belong to any church, Stuart's dreams were of a highly religious nature. As he portrayed images from his dreams onto drawings, his mother and I were startled to see that they contained various combinations of God, Baby Jesus, Mary, and a dark demonic creature. Stuart disclosed that he felt happy and protected when the Holy Family came into his dreams, but he felt quite upset when the demon appeared. He told us how the demon always followed Jesus and Mary and how he had to "fight with all his might" not to be destroyed. His rage and attempts to survive were manifesting in his aggressiveness toward family and friends.

Later, I asked Stuart to draw a picture of his family. On one side of the drawing stood Stuart and his mother. His father stood separately. Stuart appeared much larger than either of them. Through Stuart's drawings, our work moved quickly and combined the spiritual with his everyday life. First, I told Stuart he didn't have to fight with the devil anymore. Instead, when it appeared, Stuart could just tell it to leave and ask for help and protection from God, Jesus, and Mary. I explained to Stuart that it was impossible for a little boy to fight the devil all alone. But if he asked for spiritual help, he would get it. We also talked together about the family issues, and Stuart and his Mom were instructed how to create stronger boundaries between themselves.

The next time I saw Stuart, he was a different little boy. His nightmares had stopped and his anger and aggressiveness had lessened significantly. He said that when he asked for help in his dreams, the Holy Family pushed the demon away. Stuart felt that now he would always be protected. His drawing at the termination of our sessions showed a blond little boy standing between both adult-size parents and holding their hands. He was now being taken care of spiritually by God, Mary, and Baby Jesus, and psychologically by both his mom and dad.

It is important to note again that Stuart and his parents had no involvement in any church or religious activities. The spiritual nature of his dreams was not related to any personal life experiences. Typically, when adults have such experiences or dreams, they discard them with an intellectual interpretation. As a child, Stuart took his dreams seriously and, under their influence, subsequently transformed his world.

The utilization and integration of direct spiritual experience to assist in psychological and emotional development together represent the major emphasis of this new way of working and reevaluating perceptions of mental illness. The section that follows compares and contrasts existing psychological methods with this new approach.

PSYCHOLOGY AND PSYCHIATRY

Today, most emotional and personal growth work reflects the tenets and methodology adhered to by mainstream psychology and psychiatry. While there are many varied techniques used in the different branches of psychology, overall, psychology and psychiatry pay primary attention to cognitive thought processes, emotions, personality dynamics, and family-of-origin influences. While unconscious dynamics are acknowledged by some clinicians, higher states of consciousness, paranormal phenomena, and mystical connections are not. In other words, a human being is perceived as a biological organism with a brain which is primary, and emotions which are secondary. When a person dies, his body stops, and that is it. Virtually no attention is paid to spiritual consciousness, to God, or to an acknowledgment of the soul. Overall, psychiatry reflects atheistic, rationalistic, and materialistic perspectives. Our culture has certainly paralleled this world view in much of the 1970s and into the 90s.

Where does the individual who has spiritual leanings go? What about the person who feels there is more to life than a good job, happy family relationships, financial security, and good friendships? What about the existential pain that so many people feel today, a pain that is acted out through drugs and sexual promiscuity, violence toward others, mental illness, depression, or despair and suicide? More than 50 percent of married couples divorce; drug and alcohol consumption is on the rise; and families are being destroyed internally through personal turmoil, and externally through societal pressure. Have you ever considered that our institutions, experts, and leaders are not providing the real truths for which our souls are thirsting?

What happens when people turn to organized religion? Once again, people are often not really helped to connect with their souls. Many clergy will interpret the Bible to their congregations, tell people how they should live their lives, and describe what God is about. Often there is no encouragement or even acknowledgment that an individual is inherently able to receive direct guidance through ultimate wisdom.

Psychiatrists, most academics, and many mainstream clergy do not acknowledge what many people in other cultures throughout history have known. That is, we can all contact God within us and God outside of us. When we do, our own divine spark becomes ignited. When this spark is extinguished by "experts" who have no expertise, the ultimate light results in darkness.

PERCEPTIONS OF MENTAL ILLNESS

Mental and emotional disorders afflict millions of Americans each year. The most serious forms of mental illness fit under the category of psychoses. Schizophrenia and bipolar disorders are two common types of psychoses that disable an estimated three million persons annually. Theories underlying the cause of psychoses are varied and inconsistent. They include explanations based on genetics, biochemical factors, structural brain impairment, faulty family dynamics, and restrictive personality development. In fact, however, there is no clear consensus regarding cause. Diagnosis of schizophrenic conditions is also quite inconsistent and unreliable, as is the ability to predict the course of the disorder and its prognosis.

Frequently included with clinical descriptions of psychoses are references to *religious ideation*, a term assigned by psychiatry to the spiritual imagery, thoughts, and feelings regularly reported by mentally ill patients. At the same time, pioneers in the newly developing field of consciousness research have coined the term *spiritual ground* to describe a radically expanded view of consciousness resident within all human beings (rather than a by-product of the brain). However, mental health practitioners do not acknowledge the reality of a spiritual ground or understand the relevance that it has for their clients. The force of this spiritual energy will push to the surface unresolved and confused parts of the personality that need to be healed. Within psychiatry there has been no understanding of the fears that can stem from spontaneous access to these energies. Psychiatrists are trained to regard such phenomena as primary clinical indicators of mental illness.

Persons with serious mental illness, particularly those experiencing an acute episode, are usually hospitalized and given heavy doses of psychotropic medication that cause many unpleasant side effects. They may also undergo various forms of rehabilitation to assist them to live independently in the community. Such individuals rarely function independently for extended periods of time. Rather, they are subject to episodic relapses and often live in fear, panicked by the uncertainty of their shifting realities. Neither clients nor their families understand religious experiences that shift from profound fear to ecstatic imagery.

Numerous religious historians, researchers, and anthropologists have described over the centuries the role of mystics, saints, and shamans who have accessed and integrated into consciousness their accounts of direct spiritual experiences. In contemporary Western psychiatry, such descriptions are reserved for madness. On this point, Joseph Campbell has stated that "to my amazement . . . the imagery of schizophrenic fantasy perfectly matches that of the mythological hero's journey." Campbell further suggests that:

> the individual with psychosis, the mystic, the yogi and the LSD taker are all plunged into the same deep inward sea. However, the mystic endowed with native talents for this sort of thing, and following stage by stage the instruction of the master, enters the waters and finds he can swim; whereas, the schizophrenic, unprepared, unguided and ungifted, has fallen or has intentionally plunged and is drowning (p.216).

The *Diagnostic and Statistical Manual, Fourth Edition*, the standardized psychiatric reference book for diagnosis of all mental conditions, defines psychotic as follows:

> Psychotic—a term indicating gross impairment in reality testing. It may be used to describe the behavior of an individual at a given time or a [life-long] mental disorder.

The major problem with this definition of psychotic is its reference to an unspecified definition of *reality*. If an individual identifies with a reality that differs from one that a psychiatrist ascribes to, then such a person may very well be diagnosed and treated as mentally ill. Clearly, psychosis is considered the most serious of mental illness, and, as mentioned earlier, the cure rate after treatment is slight. Strong dosages of antipsychotic medication with many uncomfortable side effects are given when anyone is foolish enough to mention to a psychiatrist that she or he has had some direct contact with God or has had any other spiritual experience.

Mystical experiences can entail much fear and trauma. Despite this, one who experiences such religious contact should not be labeled mentally ill. Such a person needs spiritual guidance, support, and information. The point is not for a psychiatrist to tell a patient that her visions are unreal and then to give her medication to cover up such experiences. Rather, she should be helped to understand that she may be receiving direct information about her true nature. This information will probably be symbolic, as is the content of most mystical experiences. The emphasis of mental health professionals should not be on negating the experience but, rather, on understanding and working with the individual's personality dynamics that may make it difficult to relate to or integrate such an experience.

The larger point is that people who have spiritual experiences are not necessarily psychotic or otherwise mentally ill. When they go through a mystical experience, there is a strong probability that they will become overwhelmed if they do not have the knowledge and ego structure to know what their experience means. These people need help from someone who understands.

SPIRITUALITY GONE AWRY

The next two stories are representative of what I believe is a major crisis of our time. These accounts reflect two very serious problems that are addressed throughout the course of this book. First, they illustrate the catastrophic effect on people's lives that results from lack of communication between religious institutions and the psychiatric community. Second, they portray the limited knowledge of psychiatry regarding the true spiritual nature of all people.

Evelyn: The Odd One Out

Evelyn, an intelligent, young woman in her late twenties, had been working with me in therapy for about a year. She was engaged in a meditative practice, and I had been seeing her for her individual therapy. Evelyn was a graduate of a highly rated Ivy League university where she had earned a degree in psychology at the top of her class. The last five years for her, however, had been difficult. She discovered upon graduation from college that she did not feel comfortable working in the fast-track job that she had attained, doing psychology research for a university-connected think tank. Her interests had grown increasingly spiritual, and she felt that her job did not allow her to be herself or pursue her new set of values.

As a result of her spiritual and psychological proclivities, she decided to create a low-key lifestyle and began to live and work as a counselor and advisor in a small residential community for serious mentally ill persons. Located in an idyllic country setting, this facility proved to be an ideal experience for Evelyn. She enjoyed the natural environment, and she could use her skills and interests with the residents.

Evelyn was born Jewish and was part of a family that espoused more traditional, upper middle class values. Her father and sister were physicians, her mother a housewife. Her family identified with the traditional medical model and lived in a manner that reflected their financial prosperity and materialistic values. They also did not express religious values of any kind. Evelyn had grown up always feeling like the odd one out. Not only did she not fit in with her family concerning spiritual issues, but she vigorously rebelled against their medical orientation. For many years she had followed holistic health practices and had become macrobiotic in her eating and philosophy. As an adult her lifestyle became a continuation of the rebellion she had directed toward her family during her teenage years.

Paradoxically, because her self-esteem had not been strongly developed during childhood, she often tried to prove herself by being a perfectionist. If she planned to do something, she had to do it perfectly. After she accomplished the task in question, she would go on to the next. She often joked with me about what she called her "obsessive-compulsive" nature.

For several months she and I had been focusing on the relationship that she had just ended with her lover. This separation had been difficult for her, but she had made a decision that, I believed, would be in her best interests. The unconditional love that she believed she had received from him turned out not to be so. She had come to understand how this confusion on her part came about because she mistakenly felt that the relationship was meeting a need that her father had not met. Once Evelyn could see this and act on it, she not only gave up her attempt to fill old, unmet needs that her father had been unable to provide, but at the same time she was able to grow psychologically.

With the passing of time, Evelyn's process deepened. She began to have spiritual experiences. The first time this occurred, it seemed simplistic and confusing. One spring morning she walked into my office with a big smile on her face. "Judith," she exclaimed, "the strangest thing happened on my way over here. No sooner did I get in my car to come here, than I started to sing Christmas carols aloud and continued until I pulled my car into your driveway."

Later, Evelyn had a meditative experience in which she envisioned Christ. These experiences continued into her dreams. We spent much time talking about this in our individual sessions. As a Jew, she had a lot of trouble accepting that Christ meant something in her life. I shared my idea that Jesus represented the perfected human being—that God used Him to demonstrate to the world the human potential and how we could all ultimately be filled with God's energy as we developed spiritually and through evolution. I also suggested to her that we should each try to live out our destinies to become sons and daughters of our Creator, and to let the Christ consciousness pass through us. The challenge, I told her, was to accept this gift and live in the world in a manner whereby we give back to others the love, compassion, and truths that are being made available to us. This seemed to be helpful to Evelyn. She saw how she could use these attributes in her work, and her life opened up remarkably for a short period of time.

Her story, however, did not turn out well. Evelyn was sent to a conference through the facility where she worked. It was a large national conference held every year that presented experiential and didactic workshops on psychospiritual topics. It focused on New Age topics, and most of the presenters were well-known in their field. Evelyn walked into a workshop conducted by a well-known practitioner. Along with about forty other participants, she was led into a guided trance—no longer than fifteen minutes—that was facilitated by the workshop leader. Alone in this distant city, Evelyn had a very deep experience of Christ. The workshop leader herself had no way of knowing this, and at the end of the conference she flew off to Europe where she was holding her next workshop.

I received a call from Evelyn's coworkers several days later to tell me that Evelyn had become unable to function appropriately at work. Upon meeting with her, I discovered that she was considering admitting herself to a psychiatric hospital. Since mental hospitals symbolized to her all that was wrong in the world, she felt that becoming a patient in such a hospital would be her way of carrying out her own crucifixion, as Christ had done on the cross. She also informed me that this would be her initiation and that it was something she had to do.

Gently, but with strong conviction, I shared my thoughts with her. "Evelyn, you are acting out as a rebel again—this time toward me—as you have done all your life toward your parents. You are also being a perfectionist and compulsive again, and letting your ego get involved. You are not Christ and don't need to be crucified or to destroy yourself in the process. You've had an experience of Christ consciousness—don't fall back into your old way of feeling about yourself."

Evelyn then smiled at me and said that she was sorry, but that she had to do it her way. Saddened, I realized she had been overwhelmed by her mystical experience, and her childhood ways of conceptualizing things had come into play. Her family encouraged her decision to enter a hospital despite my efforts to dissuade them. They quickly contacted a psychiatrist, who admitted her to a hospital and started her on psychotropic medication. I realized that once the psychiatric establishment had taken over, Evelyn's care was out of my hands. Nonetheless, speaking to the psychiatrist at the hospital, I shared my thoughts about Evelyn's spiritual experiences, about how her personality dynamics were distorting a potentially transforming opportunity into one of possible destruction.

Her mother met with me three weeks after Evelyn had been hospitalized. "I wish we had listened to you, Judith," she said. "Evelyn has used up her lifelong psychotherapy insurance benefits during three weeks in the hospital—she hasn't been helped, and now they want to transfer her to a state hospital and put her on medical assistance. We've found a small institution in the Midwest where we're sending her instead. But she's extremely depressed." Five months later, Evelyn was still living at a psychiatric facility in another city.

Evelyn's story illustrates the way in which her unresolved relationship issues with her parents had a devastating effect on our work together and her travel along the spiritual path. As Evelyn replayed her childhood needs to do things her own way, my ability to guide her on her spiritual path was diminished. This new way of working necessitates that the client not confuse the therapist with his or her mother or father. When old family issues come up, they must be strongly confronted and put aside. In retrospect, I should have addressed Evelyn's transference issues more strongly than I did. My training as a psychologist was clearly getting in the way.

Another serious problem that befell Evelyn was her experience in the workshop at the New Age conference she attended. The workshop leader did not recognize the magnitude of the spiritual energies that were triggered in Evelyn. If the leader had recognized their potential, perhaps she wouldn't have brought them to the surface in such a nonchalant way.

Both factors—Evelyn's unresolved personality dynamics and the workshop leader's seeming lack of understanding about the effects of this person's spiritual experiences—contributed to the crisis. The most critical problem, however, was and is, psychiatry's total lack of knowledge regarding Evelyn's problem. There was no professional in the psychiatric hospital who understood Evelyn's process or who could help her come to terms with anything that was happening. The perceptions I shared with the doctor in charge were ignored and not understood.

Penny: Was I Insane?

Penny was in the audience during a presentation I made on my work at a mental health conference in Pittsburgh in 1992. Following are excerpts from a letter she sent me after the conference.

Dear Judy,

> *I attended your presentation at the conference. I was one of the people who came up to speak with you afterwards. It's important for me to tell you that as soon as I get symptomatic, certain "themes" often begin, themes you mentioned in your talk . . . found in spiritual traditions around the world. . . . My diagnosis is bipolar disorder. I have been interested in metaphysics since my early 20s. I am now in my late 40s. Maybe that is why I understood my illness in terms of spirituality or mysti-*

cism. All I can say is that synchronicity is a rather common occurrence to me.

What happens with people who are "symptomatic" is that they read into everything. What I mean by this is that they know that there is a direct connection between thoughts and physical manifestations and vice versa. . . . Also, what I want you to know is that it is almost impossible for a person to put what they are experiencing into words. . . . This feels like it has cosmic effects when the theme is good and evil.

Again, thank you for your presentation. It was a very emotional experience for me. I felt as though someone finally understood. It was all I could do to keep from crying.

Sincerely, Penny

Penny enclosed with this letter something she had written in April of 1992:.

It is time I worked out the pain involved in my hospital commitment hearing. . . . I know there is an agreed-upon reality. Society deals harshly with those who do not stay within it. They are isolated, stigmatized, feared and dehumanized. That is why with every fiber of my being and with every resource at my command, I try to stay within those boundaries. . . . .

The only people at the hearing were men . . . my father and son were there, but did not testify. The man who was my husband at the time testified against me. . . . The rest of those present were strangers. What was I to do?

That was the commitment hearing. Feelings of powerlessness, yes. Feelings of betrayal, yes. The betrayal was by society. My former husband only followed the mandates dictated by that society. What the commitment hearing symbolized and asked me to give up was the identification with . . . awareness. It asked me to deny it. I am asked to label it insanity and not acknowledge it.

But others have experienced this intense awareness and are experiencing it now. I recognize the language and symbols when I hear it from the "crazies" in the streets and in the psychiatric hospitals. People in support groups gingerly refer to it and laugh. What is it, a mass hallucination?

Was I insane? I don't know. What I did know was that the second reality was absorbed and experienced by me with an intensity of feelings and thought. . . . In the past I have phrased the second reality as another level of consciousness, but now the term intense awareness seems more accurate. . . . Mood, intent, harmony, disharmony, the yin and yang, the ebb and flow and all that comprise it, including music, sound, vibration, movement, the earth elements, color texture, energy, love, fear, tenderness and all the human emotions. It was not only an intense awareness, but an awareness of the root of all, including the mysterious, the unknown, and the magical forces.

My time spent sleeping and dreaming was as real as my waking hours. I can remember the dreams, including the sensations and feelings associated with them as if it were yesterday. While awake or asleep (and it's difficult to separate the two), I entered and went beyond ecstasy, ending all thoughts and feelings of separateness. All is one. I traveled through the seven realms of hell, each one being more emotionally painful, but yet more commonplace then the next. . . .

I have learned not to speak of it . . . in the telling, it is *impossible to separate the pain of its stigma from the actual experience itself. . . .*

It was a gift, a gift reserved for "crazies" and mystics.

Penny Perlman is currently working as a lay advocate for the mentally ill. She is also the director of an information clearinghouse for people needing mental health services.

The day that I was writing this chapter, another letter arrived, this one from a person who had been unable to attend a conference I had recently conducted in Monticello, New York:

Dear Judith Miller,

Hello, my name is Stella, and . . . I was unable to make the conference although I really wanted to go and meet you. Some of my working pals were able to go and they provided me with your paper. The paper was so amazing, I had to take it in small doses. . . . the list for defining a mystical experience and the concept of synchronicity were all hitting home. . . . I am by no means a "religious zealot" or "fanatic," but my faith in God has been heightened and deepened by a "communion" of sorts with a spiritual world.

I am currently putting together a sequence of events starting from the onset of psychosis to the recovery process, which has been over seven years. I am leaving out the "symbolic" life involved in psychosis for fear some would not understand. Can you correspond with me for a bit so I can develop some validation on this matter?

Yours truly, Stella

I have come to understand human nature in ways that are very different from my colleagues' understanding. My awareness has come from my clients, from those who have come up to me or written to me after my conference presentations, and from my own direct connection. Through my work, I guide people to expand their worlds, and once they make their own direct connection, their lives unfold in miraculous ways. I have come to believe that traveling such a path represents a higher form of human consciousness than most people achieve. But I have also become aware that this expanded consciousness is now being experienced by growing numbers of people. This book, through my personal story, points the way to an expanded consciousness.

There is an order and purpose for each of our lives.

CHAPTER 2

In the Beginning

The world is very different for me now from what it was in the past. Yesterday, I looked outside myself for the truth. Today, I contact reality directly through my deepest self. Now I know that when we connect with the universal wisdom that resides within, we can experience the past, present, and future in a single moment. The people I work with have also come to know this. As I guide them to an expanded state of consciousness, they understand that when they trust themselves, they have nothing to fear. Moreover, they have found themselves on a path that continues to open to higher realms of consciousness and expanded reality. Along this journey their psychological well-being continues to improve.

In 1980, I completed my graduate studies with a doctoral degree in psychology from Temple University. While I once worked as a mainstream psychologist, now I work with people nontraditionally. This dramatic shift reflects my own journey and integrates modern psychological theory and techniques with ancient practices that have been found in many cultures around the world.

Through my extensive studies over the past twenty years, as well as through the direct experiences of my clients and those of my own life, I can assert with conviction that we all are able to access a greater wisdom regarding the meaning of existence. We can develop powers that truly enlarge our worlds.

A CHILDHOOD EXPERIENCE

Born in the middle of World War II and growing up in the 1950s, I experienced material plenty, conservatism, "the organization man," and acceptance of rational, mechanistic values. As the 1960s unfolded, my heart and passions identified with those who worked to bring our world closer to Utopia. The intensity and deep meaning of those days still remain with me, so much so that I believe my strong motivation to expand people's consciousness stems in large part from living through those very exhilarating, turbulent times.

Although I identified with no particular religious practices or beliefs while growing up, my family was Jewish and we attended synagogue on special holidays. In addition, my brother and I went to Hebrew school for many years, but I found no emotional connection there. Through high school and college, I turned away from religion and identified myself as either an agnostic or an atheist.

When I was a young girl, one of my teachers remarked that I often daydreamed and gazed out the window. Even then I found more excitement in my inner world than in the external environment. I also vividly recall a precognitive experience that occurred when I was ten years old, before my family was to move to Florida. While in bed preparing for sleep, I visualized my best friend, Eva, coming to me in school and inviting me to her house for dinner. Walking up the steps to her front door, I rang the bell, saw her mother open the door, and, from a darkened living room, heard all my friends shouting "surprise." This was to be a going-away party before my family moved to Florida. Next, I saw that we ate dinner and afterwards played a game called "This is Your Life," a popular television show of the time. In this game, each of my friends enacted an aspect of my life.

The next day at school—in real life—Eva invited me to her house for dinner. As I climbed the steps to her front door that evening, her mother met me, and my friends shouted from the darkened living room. After dinner, I was not surprised when we began to play "This is Your Life."

Precognition—the sensing, sight, or knowledge of a future occurrence—is common. Hunches and intuition are words that are often used to describe aspects of precognition. If we consider the implications of precognition as we try to understand life, questions about the nature of time and space, the extent to which our lives are fated, and the role of free will, will necessarily be raised.

As a child, I viewed my precognitive experience as quite natural. I also did not think much about such things as a teenager. It felt more important to engage in emotional highs and lows over boyfriends. My interest in academic subjects remained rather minimal, and I could not get excited over things other than my interpersonal dramas. If any thoughts lingered over events such as Eva's party, they were minimal at best, and for the most part I simply did not deal with them.

As an adult and a psychologist trained in scientific methods, I have come to assume a different attitude about Eva's party. By itself, the incident can easily be explained—coincidence, perhaps. But Eva's party was not an isolated incident. Throughout my adult years I continued to experience such nonordinary events with increased frequency, intensity, and variety.

EARLY ADULTHOOD

Getting married during my sophomore year of college at the advanced age of nineteen seemed to be the thing to do at the time. I then completed college, taught third grade for several years, and "retired" when my first child, Philip, was born. Three years later Marjorie was born, and along with raising a baby and a toddler, I taught school as a substitute teacher, became a volunteer tour guide at the Philadelphia Art Museum, and practiced oil painting. This was my phase as an artist. Our home and those of my friends and relatives still display examples from this period of my life. I recall moments during those years when I would lose myself as I painted—when time, space, and my surroundings would fade into the background as I felt surges of excitement around newly discovered colors and shapes that appeared on my palette and canvas boards.

Most artists experience this sensation of losing themselves in their work at times. Our language describes the process as creativity. How is this process different from other nonordinary events in which objective reality no longer seems to matter? Our culture, like the field of psychiatry, often uses words to define nonordinary events in ways that, at best, do not do justice to the experience and, at worst, label the experience in such negative terms as mental illness.

Meanwhile, the Vietnam War, civil rights demonstrations, and women's consciousness-raising continued. Society appeared to be bursting at the seams. My personal life paralleled the times. On the one hand, I felt happy and serene. But while my budding artistic talents developed and my new family provided me with joy, I experienced the loss of childhood security—my parents divorced after thirty years of marriage.

Suddenly, the traditional middle class values and standards of an appropriate lifestyle with which I had grown up no longer worked. My parents' individual and collective pain became my pain, until I realized that I was, in fact, a separate person and needed to live my life in a way that represented who I was as opposed to who they were. Their divorce, in combination with the turbulent times and my own emotional shifts, moved me to start reading books on psychology and self-development. Amid this combination of reading and self-exploration, I applied to graduate school to study psychology.

Being a psychologist is my life's work. I consider myself fortunate because this work incorporates my deepest convictions and provides me with an opportunity to act on these convictions in the world. An important aspect of my work in graduate school consisted of clinical counseling with clients. Such counseling, done under supervision, is called a practicum or internship. My first experience was in a prison, where I worked half-time for a year. There I learned that I could accept and work with people who had murdered, raped, or engaged in other violent crimes. I discovered that beneath the inmates' hardened exteriors, their feelings and emotions were similar to mine. It was at the prison that I became aware for the first time of a prevailing humanness shared by all people that transcends race and socioeconomic background. Underlying emotions are the same for all people, although these emotions can be expressed differently and to various degrees.

My second placement was at Horizon House, a rehabilitation center for people with serious psychiatric difficulties. (This experience led to a therapist's job one year later.) At Horizon House I focused primarily on helping former mental patients to live and work independently in the community. The year was 1974, and this institution was a leading, nationally respected rehabilitation center. As did others in the field, Horizon House operated under the philosophy that people who had suffered serious mental illness needed support and external structure to feel accepted. They also needed practical assistance to live and work in the community and to develop improved interpersonal and social skills. It was a behavior-modifying approach which promoted the belief that support, consistency, and re-education, when combined with antipsychotic medication, would enable the individual to function effectively in the community. This approach began as a radical departure from the fifty-minute, once-a-week session in the psychiatrist's office. In the 1980s and 90s, it has become the leading method of treatment for those who have been termed "long-term mentally ill."

My work with this population also helped me recognize the universality of emotions. As far back as 1974, I realized that a diagnosis of schizophrenia did not diminish the fact that in many basic ways we are all alike. Even though cognitive processes and emotional expression may differ among us, the core humanness deep within each of us is not very separate or distinct from one person to the next.

During my four years at Horizon House, my counseling with clients differed from that of my colleagues. I paid less attention to outer behavior, focusing instead on the underlying feelings and inner worlds of my clients. Whether their inner worlds felt frightening, confusing, or exhilarating, I guided them to work through these feelings and was pleased with the successes we achieved. My supervisor noticed this and increasingly assigned to me those individuals he thought had the most serious psychiatric problems.

My manner of working with persons who were diagnosed as psychotic clearly did not follow the accepted mode. However, since my clients appeared to make steady progress there were no complaints. During this phase of my career I operated intuitively, without fully conceptualized theoretical perspectives or treatment practices regarding mental illness. At this time I was impressed that my clients' experiences of voices and other "hallucinations" were not all that different from some of my own "unusual" experiences.

One afternoon I was home alone, sitting in the living room studying for a statistics exam. Never liking mathematics very much, I felt quite insecure with all those complex formulas. In the midst of this, I remember hearing a deep male voice that said, "Hello, Judy." Although this voice sounded assuring, strong, and kind, I was startled and then scared. I checked to make sure that no one was around, and, finding this to be the case, I tried not to think about it and went back to studying.

Years later I became aware of a phenomenon called clairaudience. Clairaudience means hearing by paranormal means. Telepathic messages are "heard" in an internalized way. The voices may be either recognized or unfamiliar. People who report hearing such voices (whether to the side, above, or within their heads) are often identified as mediums, sensitives, or psychics. Such a person can be described as an intermediary for communication between the material and spiritual world. Clearly many people—particularly, psychiatrists—would ridicule and dismiss these explanations. Individuals who may have had such an experience may also attempt to push it away, pretend it never happened, or dismiss it as just belonging to their imagination. To acknowledge such an experience would bring up a fear of serious mental illness and would certainly challenge the consensus reality in which they live. Yet scholars and scientists have studied such things through established empirical methods and have offered research findings that confirm these abilities.

Epiphenomena

During this period I had a major experience that catapulted me on the journey that I am still traveling. It began after an uneventful day, while I was in bed on a Friday night, gently moving into sleep. I could be described as being in a hypnagogic state, which occurs when one rests drowsily between sleeping and waking. Whatever comes into one's awareness at this time tends to be spontaneous, usually meaningful, and not necessarily linked to any conscious thoughts or experiences. My husband, Marty, was sleeping next to me, and my children, Marjorie and Philip, were each asleep in their bedrooms down the hall.

As my eyes closed I became aware of a tugging on the right side of my body. Although this occurred many years ago, I still remember with great detail and clarity the *feeling* of this experience. The tugging shifted into a strong pull. With effort, I tried to hold myself together so that I would not be propelled out of my body. I felt that if I let go, allowing myself to fly away, I would die.

As this happened, an entirely unfamiliar word sped repeatedly through my mind: "epiphenomena." Even as the word raced uncontrollably through the left side of my brain, the pulling on the right side of my body intensified. I am not sure how long this process lasted. It could have been a few minutes or many hours—my awareness of time and space felt distorted, and my mind seemed out of control. I could not suppress this word, although it felt so intrusive and unfamiliar. I remained in a state of intense fear, feeling that I would die if I let down my guard and flew out of my body. Despite this fear I was unable to turn to Marty to ask for help, unable even to sit up or move. I was in a trance state, a type of paralysis. I clearly remember the moment that the pulling stopped, and I knew then that the insistent repetition of the word *epiphenomena* would also stop, as it did. When I awakened from this state, I related the entire incident to my husband, including the repetition of the unfamiliar word.

On Saturdays I was usually busy with errands, but on this Saturday I found I needed to stay in bed. I was not thinking of the experience of the night before; I just felt too weak to get up. I had an image that a heavy truck had run over me. Around 4:00 P.M. I was suddenly energized. I got out of bed and began to function. At dinner that evening, Philip asked why I had been in bed all day. While telling the events of my strange night, I was now unable to recall the strange word. Over the years I have noticed that when startling paranormal experiences occur, I often have a tendency to repress these events beneath my conscious awareness, only to recall them after the emotional shock has diminished.

Marty, however, remembered that I had told him the word was *epiphenomena*. At this point we looked up the word in the dictionary. First, the singular noun *epiphenomenon* was described as a "secondary phenomenon accompanying another and caused by it." Following this definition was an entry for *epiphenomenalism*, defined as a doctrine stating that mental processes are epiphenomena of brain processes.

The doctrine of epiphenomenalism is representative of a traditional view which sees consciousness as directly related to physiological processes within the brain. This conceptual view seeks to explain such phenomena as human intelligence, creativity, art, religion, and ethics solely as products of physical processes of the brain. Although close correlations exist between consciousness and cerebral structures, the interpretations currently offered by traditional science are open to question. However, a new relationship between physics and the nature of consciousness and mental processes is being recognized by physicists. This new theory of the universe describes the world we observe in our ordinary state of consciousness as representing only a partial aspect of reality. There is another level of reality that cannot be observed directly except possibly in nonordinary consciousness, such as deep meditative and mystical states. This assumption challenges the existing systems of scientific and medical thought. It also opens new perspectives for speculation about mystical states, spiritual awakenings, and other areas that had previously been excluded from the study of human psychology.

It is important to emphasize the significance that my *epiphenomena* experience has had for me through the years. It clearly shook my conception of the world and my place in it. Upon reading in the dictionary that epiphenomenalism deals with the relationship between consciousness and the brain, my heart started beating rapidly as I began to see the ways in which this definition paralleled my experience. The experience had caused me to feel split, the right side of my brain believing that my deepest and most core sense of self was about to fly away and leave my body. The left side of my brain had accessed a word of which, at the time, I had no knowledge, a word whose meaning embedded contemporary academic Western thought. The conflict within me was a conflict between the abstract, non-material, intuitive right side of my brain and the rational, mechanistic, cognitive thought processes of the left. Suddenly the concept of mind-brain-body relationship, a concept that I had never before considered, became the major focus of my life.

At that moment of personal revelation, I heard a loud knocking that seemed to reverberate through the house. We all heard it—Marjie started to cry, my dog began to bark. It was an acknowledgment that a journey was to begin for me—a journey that was to change my life, my work, and my view of the world in ways that I could never have imagined. My immediate reaction was fear of the unknown. What was going on? What was reality, anyway?

The twenty years since the *epiphenomena* experience have been profound. Throughout these years my life has been transformed in a manner that paralleled the split that I felt in that experience. Being a professional, contemporary woman functioning as a psychologist, college professor, wife, mother, and daughter has contrasted with that other side of me, the one traveling in deep inner spaces which, at best, have felt magical, mystical, and surrealistic—and, at worst, quite crazy. These years in my life have evolved into a private journey that has been my attempt to bridge that split and to make my world whole.

After I received my doctoral degree in 1980, I experienced another extraordinary phenomenon. One night as I was sleeping, a sudden energy moved rapidly through my body. As the energy traveled to my head, I heard a popping sound and became aware of myself flying through the air and out the window, landing next to the big tree that I enjoyed looking at from my bedroom. Whereas during the *epiphenomena* experience I had felt that I had a choice to prevent myself from leaving my body, now I had no choice. The energy raced through so rapidly that it seemed as though my core self was actually flying through the air. Since there was no time for fear, I found myself next to the tree, wanting to come back inside.

Because Marty was out of town, I began to call, in my mind, for Marjorie to help me come back inside the house. No sooner had these thoughts coursed through my head than I found myself back in my body in my bed. I immediately returned to sleep and felt quite happy on awakening the next morning. How shocking, how liberating this experience was! My previous fears of leaving my body, of dying and not coming back, were now gone. I had an out-of-body experience in spite of myself. And it felt wonderful to fly.

MY PERSPECTIVES TODAY

Before I proceed with further details of my journey, it may be helpful to review briefly some of the perspectives I now hold. First, my perception of the world and my place in it is without boundaries. I view life and death as being on a continuum. When our physical body dies, our essence—the core self, or soul—continues, and may do so in myriad ways.

I cannot fault the skeptical reader who challenges my statements and demands proof, proof that certainly must seem unattainable as I speak of after-death experiences in a very much alive state. Interpretations stemming from my journey come from direct experience and extensive study. The 20th-century's idealized notion of the scientific method is quite limited, I believe, and was developed by persons who are convinced that life's mysteries can best be understood and controlled by a formula that people have invented.

As I continue to describe my thoughts and experiences, I will do so knowing that most readers who have not shared such phenomena will find it hard to understand and will question my credibility. I can accept this attitude because I recognize that the consensus reality of 20th-century Western culture is different from the one that I describe in this book. However, I am hopeful that my experiences and interpretations will prove useful to those who may have had their own unusual experiences, but who have so far repressed them for lack of a context in which to place them. For those individuals whose experiences have been labeled psychotic, I ask that you rethink your diagnosis as you learn of my journey. In sum, I hope that my experiences will enable all readers to trust themselves more and to think about themselves in new, nonthreatening and constructive ways.

My journey over these years, I should emphasize, has been benevolent and purposeful. Although I have had some difficult times, the process has unfolded in a manner that I could handle-one that never became too overwhelming. As a clinical psychologist, I was all too aware that traditional psychiatry would have regarded many of my experiences as pathologic. This fact has created a troublesome challenge I have had to overcome over the years. How paradoxical that the professional discipline of which I am a part, operates on principles and uses methods that I now believe can be, for many, detrimental to good mental health. Despite psychiatry's perceptions, I have subsequently learned that many cultures, spiritual beliefs, and traditions that have been practiced around the world through the ages support experiences of expanded consciousness. Increasingly, many people today in Western society find themselves shifting into altered states of consciousness. They feel their consciousness to be radically different from its ordinary functional state. They are engaged in a process that takes them beyond the material world as we know it. Some people, for example, find themselves knowing a few minutes before the phone rings that a particular person will call. This is a common, everyday example of precognition. Because the implications of such an experience are unsettling, very often the individual will repress it or even scoff at it.

The consequences of this defensive behavior are twofold. First, the individual is stultifying an opportunity to expand his or her understanding of human nature and, as a result, is passing up an opportunity to move in the direction of fuller emotional empowerment and development. Second, when awareness is covered up, society is held back because it remains stuck in a limiting world view.

There are numerous types of paranormal experiences that people can have. Among these are: accurate telepathic reading of other people's thoughts; clairvoyance, the ability to discern objects not present to the senses; and out-of-body experiences (OBEs), in which the consciousness seems to separate itself from the body so that the individual can see him or herself from above or from a distance. OBEs have repeatedly been experienced by persons very close to death, but they also occur when a person is healthy. After experiencing many paranormal phenomena, I have accepted that reality for me has changed permanently. It is important to understand the inherent meaning of paranormal experiences. Such experiences help us clarify what reality is and is not. When our lives begin to feel magical, we may find it increasingly difficult to identify with the narrow limits and constraints of 20th-century Western culture.

One strong caution, however: avoid ego inflation over what may seem like new powers. As people glimpse and learn to access expanded reality, they will, ideally, learn from it in a manner that will ultimately help their society. Unfortunately, some try to use these abilities to exploit others or to engage in power games. Not only can this be harmful, it can also cut short the growth process of the person who betrays such a gift in exchange for personal gain.

What Is Spiritual Consciousness?

It is important to note that people often confuse paranormal events with "spirituality." Some equate spirituality with organized religion, others with "morality" as postulated by society, and still others combine psychic states with spiritual practices and then translate it all into a "New Age" package that entices some and creates scorn and ridicule in others.

Society is moving toward a spiritual revolution. Tension has grown between those who hold a pragmatic, scientific-oriented, high-tech approach to life, and those whose beliefs emphasize such varied credos as religious fundamentalism, "born again" Christianity, and New Age utopia.

What is the relationship between psychic phenomena and spirituality, and why have they become so closely linked? From my perspective, the connection comes about because both categories of experience are part of what has been referred to as an expanded reality that goes beyond Western society's tunnel vision. Such nonordinary states of consciousness as out-of-body experiences, telepathy, being bathed in transcendental white light, or miracle healing, all seem to tap into a continuum that crosses traditional time-space boundaries as defined by scientific thought.

The development of psychic abilities can result in an expanded world view. To become truly spiritual, however, means to change radically one's entire personality, and with such change the realization that this material world is only one part of total existence. For me, spirituality involves feeling connected to nature, animals, and my fellow humans. It means to experience this connection as a wheel that keeps rolling, making contact with everything it touches in ever-changing, important ways. Further, while I see the pain, violence, and darkness in the world, I must live as fully as I can in the beauty, love, and light, which are far more prevalent.

When the spiritual energy force attaches to our fears, it can become very disruptive if we don't understand what is happening. Only through recognizing and challenging our personal shadows can we, both individually and collectively, clear ourselves and remove the barriers that prevent us from reaching our potential. We can begin to move in this direction if we try to live our lives in a truthful manner, one in which compromises and rationalizations are acknowledged. We must work toward a life of integrity based on ethical principles and values. We need to love ourselves in a way that permits us unconditionally to love others.

Above all, spirituality is an intimate connection to God. This includes all of the aspects mentioned above as well as deep mystical experiences that, for me, have included brilliant lights, colors, and symbols behind closed eyes. It means knowing that random accidental events no longer happen, but rather that life is purposeful and ordered. It means that I can live in the moment, never knowing what my future will be, knowing only that I must follow a path that somehow has been laid out for me. It means acknowledging my human weaknesses and knowing ultimately that I have only limited control—but knowing also that a higher force and meaning are with me to ensure that I'll never again be alone.

The core self or soul survives forever. After a long process of development—incorporating many lives—it will eventually perfect itself. Sometimes a soul may exist in another realm in spirit form.

CHAPTER 3
The Art of Dying

Throughout my adult life, a number of experiences have shown me that the physical death of our bodies is both an ending and a beginning. The ending relates to the dissolution of life as we have known it; the beginning, which varies in the form that it takes, represents the next unique step of the spiritual journey.

My understanding of life after death has come primarily from encounters I have had with others—both before and after their deaths. These encounters occurred over a span of years. In spite of their startling nature, my day-to-day life continued as normal. I slowly absorbed the meaning of what was happening, but did so in a gentle manner that enlarged my world view.

EARLY THOUGHTS OF DEATH

When I was sixteen years old, I awoke one morning and for no reason I know began to think about how I and the people I cared about would eventually die. I wondered why people beyond middle age are not overwhelmed by the knowledge that the years they have left are fewer than the number they have already lived. What *was* death? And what could life be if we would all end up in the ground, or as ashes, and everything we ever were, had experienced, or had learned would one day suddenly disappear? And how could older people be content, knowing that they were getting close to that time when they would disappear forever? If this was what inevitably happened, what was the purpose of living? It was difficult for me to understand why everyone did not think the way I was thinking. Or, if they did, why weren't these things discussed more?

Although resolving this issue seemed futile, I continued to ponder the meaning of life. But time moves rapidly during teenage years, and before I knew it I went to college, got married, taught elementary school, and then became pregnant with Philip. The grandparents with whom I was close were my father's parents, and during my growing-up years I spent a great deal of time and shared much fun and love with "Mom-Mom" and "Pop-Pop." During the early years of my marriage Pop-Pop was afflicted with Parkinson's disease. This led to palsy, which was an embarrassment for a proud man. In spite of his increasing withdrawal from life, he nonetheless felt excited about the prospect of his first great-grandchild.

Pop-Pop eventually could no longer live at home. As he was taken by ambulance to the nursing home, tears ran down his face. The day after his arrival there he closed his eyes and died, four months before the birth of my son Philip, who was named after him.

Doctoral Dissertation

From the first day of graduate studies, I knew that for my dissertation I wanted to focus on people's attitudes toward their own mortality. Although my existential angst regarding death had moved below the surface of my consciousness since that brief eruption during my sixteenth year, it remained for me a deep, unresolved issue. In the carefully constructed research design of my dissertation, I did not choose the topic of death anxiety casually; this choice symbolized my long-held questions about the nature of existence, reality, and mortality.

In my dissertation I studied attitudes toward death and identified such attitudes as an aspect of personality. An interesting outcome of my research demonstrated that medical students have a higher level of death anxiety than do law, accounting, and seminary students. The implications of this are significant regarding both motives for becoming a doctor, and possible effects on patient care. Are some motivated to become physicians, at least in part, to help contain their fears of their own mortality? If this is true, wouldn't such fears influence the way that doctors deal with terminally ill patients and their relatives?

Although my dissertation was accepted, this work did not come close to addressing my questions concerning the meaning of life and death. These questions, which had seemed like quiet embers, have become fiery coals over the years.

Mom-Mom

Several years before I completed my dissertation, my grandmother died. I was fortunate to be at Mom-Mom's side in the hospital when she died.

That night, as I lay in bed thinking of this dear old lady, I wondered where she was. Did her spirit or soul survive her body? I tried to communicate with my grandmother. "Mom-Mom," I thought, "can you hear me? If you can, please give me a signal." At that exact moment a flash of light moved rapidly across the room. I challenged this in my mind; I questioned whether it was anything more than a firefly. But three loud knocks suddenly reverberated on the wall of my bedroom. My eyes filled with tears, and I was awed to know that at that moment Mom-Mom was with me. I was assured that she was fine, and as my lids grew heavy and I drifted into sleep, I knew that she had given me a gift that would remain with me for the rest of my life.

During the days that followed, I wondered if this incident really happened. How did her spirit know that I was questioning her well-being at that moment? Where would she go as time passed? Was she still near me or had she moved on to another place?

As I recount this event, I have to wonder whether anyone reading this has ever had a similar experience with someone close who has died? If you have, how did you process your experience? Did you discuss it with anyone else, or did you dismiss it as "craziness"?

NEAR-DEATH EXPERIENCES

During the 1980s, my "unusual experiences" seemed to increase. Around this time I read a brochure about the International Association of Near-Death Studies (IANDS). Their literature included general descriptions of the near-death experience. Raymond Moody, a psychiatrist who coined the term "near-death experience" (NDE), was impressed with a cluster of similarities among adults and children who claimed to have had such an experience. A typical

NDE, he observed, might include one or all of the following events: at the moment of death the person will feel peace and extreme well-being and then "leave" the body, often observing the activities and emotions of others who may be tending that body. A sense that one is rapidly moving through a dark tunnel may also be present—and, once there, the person often sees a small, radiant, white light; at times the light becomes larger and engulfs the person so that there is an ineffable sense that one is merging with God.

Some NDE experiencers communicate with deceased relatives; others meet with religious figures. The information they receive often gives them universal understanding about existence as well as personal meaning of their individual lives. Another type of experience, called a "life review," is also often encountered. Here the person is enabled to observe, impartially and nonjudgmentally, virtually every action and thought in which he or she has engaged. This review seems to occur in a flash-beyond time or space—and results in a positive new understanding. Eventually the NDE experiencer becomes aware that this journey is over and he or she must return to earth, with a clear, given message that it is not yet time to cross the dividing line between earthly life and the next life. And then the NDE experiencer comes back to consensus reality in a new way.

I decided to join IANDS, which had a national and international membership. This organization was composed of professionals in the health care system, including psychologists and psychiatrists, researchers, near-death experiencers, and interested others.

It was comforting to learn about a group housed at a university that explored areas closely related to my own experiences, because these experiences, while wondrous in many ways, also made me feel alienated from the people around me. Certainly at that time, the mental health professions, at best, ignored such phenomena and, at worst, labeled them as crazy. My position in

IANDS as the Coordinator/President of the Philadelphia chapter enabled me to explore the field in more depth, to meet and work with many near-death experiencers both locally and nationally, and four years later to become a member of IANDS' national Board of Directors.

At about the same time, I began to appear on numerous television and radio programs and to speak as a psychologist on my interpretations of these experiences. When asked by interviewers if I had ever had a near-death experience, I comfortably answered that I had not. This allowed me to be heard as an objective and scientific professional. I continued to spend most of my professional life in mainstream psychology, living in the world in a manner that largely reflected American society of the 1980s. But my counseling work with near-death experiencers proved to be the most meaningful aspect of my professional life during this time.

Notwithstanding the varying ages, socioeconomic backgrounds, and religious and gender differences of NDE experiencers, the similarities in personality changes reported by people after an NDE was remarkable. They almost always lost their fear of death and gained a strong belief in the continuation of life after death. While their belief in God and spirituality strengthened, their active participation in mainstream religion typically diminished. Additionally, experiencers report developing a greater appreciation for life and for nature, together with more compassion and love, a lessened interest in materialism, and an expanded feeling of universal love and acceptance.

Many people have shared their meaningful encounters of the pivotal point between life and death with me. I am very grateful for their honesty and openness and would like to share a few of their stories.

Kimberly: A Reunion of the Highest Order

Kimberly Clark Sharp, author of *After the Light*, had her near-death experience at age twenty-two when she collapsed outside an office building in Kansas City and lay on the sidewalk:

> *I found myself surrounded by dense, warm, foggy, gray material. In the fog I could see individual droplets of penetrating lightness and droplets of unfathomable darkness. Suddenly, there was an explosion under me, and reaching out to the farthest limits of my view was this light. It was absolutely alive, in a greater sense than we experience aliveness. It was so bright, the sun is not as bright, yet it didn't hurt my eyes. It filled up everything, and I was in the center of it. I was back with my creator. The light was all love, there was nothing there but love of the greatest intensity. I was receiving information, in a communication between myself and the light, and I understood everything I was told: what is life, why we are born, universal kinds of knowledge. Profound, but there was a simplicity to it. It was like something I had known but had forgotten. It was heaven, more than ecstasy. It was a reunion of the highest order.* (Life magazine, March 1992)

It seems paradoxical that an NDE experiencer would desire or need counseling of any sort after describing such a beatific scene. Two examples come to mind that may help clarify this issue.

Bertha: The Gift of Self

Bertha, an eighty-year-old woman, came to see me several times.

She had her near-death experience during a heart attack. She told her doctor about the tunnel, the light, and her conversation with her long-deceased father; the doctor referred her to the hospital's psychiatric unit. After she was discharged from the hospital, her husband of 65 years and her children were condescending and patronizing regarding her experience, and they encouraged her to take the tranquilizers prescribed at the hospital.

A television program which Bertha saw that discussed both IANDS and the NDE helped her maintain her equilibrium. She attended several local IANDS meetings, where her experience was affirmed. However, doctors and family continued to discredit what had been the most profound event of her life. Worse, they considered her psychiatrically disturbed. While this was going on, she became aware that her husband had grown emotionally abusive toward her. Since her near-death experience she could no longer relate to him in the passive-victim role into which she had fallen during the many years of their marriage.

After several intense sessions with me, Bertha announced to her shocked family that she wanted to live independently in her own small apartment, away from her domineering, insensitive husband. Amazingly, she accomplished this quickly, even while confronting both the anger and outrage of family and friends as well as her own financial hardship.

Bertha lived the next two years of her life alone in a state of peaceful happiness. After her NDE, she gained an inner strength and courage that allowed her to go to IANDS meetings, read, and listen to music. Most of the people in her environment could not understand her new strength. As a counselor, I assisted her to make the choices that were right for her and to help her use the NDE as a learning tool in the process.

After Bertha died, her daughter called me to say that her mother had lived in a serene manner during these last few years. She also added that the family had slowly come to realize that her mother's experience had been a gift that finally allowed her to be herself for possibly the first time in her life.

Mike: A Gold Bracelet

A second, brief example of how a near-death experience can change a person is that of Mike, a fifty-year-old pharmacist from Ohio. Mike's NDE also occurred following a heart attack. He had been an upwardly mobile professional who had known success, financial ease, and family support throughout his life. He and his wife enjoyed many luxuries that came from hard work and rewarded motivation.

Mike contacted me, practically in tears, shortly after he came home from the hospital. "How could my wife give me a gold bracelet to welcome me home from the hospital?" he cried. "How can I accept a materialistic object after what I have been through?"

Clearly Mike's value system, attitudes, and even his personality had radically changed after his near-death experience. His wife continued to relate to him as she had done during all their years together. She hadn't changed—he had.

Barbara: On a Mission

Barbara Harris Whitfield, another near-death experiencer and author of *Full Circle* and *Spiritual Awakenings*, has discussed how her transformation took her by surprise. "Before my NDE," she says, "I was a sophisticated, modern, scientific atheist. Sometimes now I feel as if I am on a mission from God! Oh boy, does that sound wacky," she says, laughing. "I don't have a belief in God. I have a direct knowledge of His love."

Barbara's new-found self-esteem required her to make painful choices and changes in her life. Her marriage to a traditional husband ended, and she left her life in a wealthy suburb to become a respiratory therapist so that she could work with sick people. "I left behind a lot of financial security, but the spiritual security I was finding inside me was much more solid." (*McCall's* magazine, February 1988).

Contact after Death

Pop-Pop: A Visitation

In 1985, my involvement with IANDS was at its peak. At the same time I was very busy in my career as I traveled around the country training mental health workers in the area of psychiatric rehabilitation, lecturing, and consulting with various human service departments and agencies. A trip to train mental health workers in Fredericksburg, Virginia, stands out in my mind. As I slept one night in a motel there, I recall having a vivid dream about my grandfather Pop-Pop, who had died twenty years earlier. In the dream he appeared as a young man, which was very different from the way I remembered him. He looked strong, handsome and very much like an old photograph that I recalled seeing. He gave me advice about a very troublesome relationship with which I was having problems at the time.

Suddenly I felt fear. As I slowly began to shift from a dream state to one of wakefulness, I became aware of Pop-Pop's presence in the room, a presence so strong that I could not deny it. This sense evolved into a feeling of love that seemed to fill the motel room and was stronger and unlike anything I had ever experienced during my lifetime. It was so intense that it felt physical, but physical beyond the senses, beyond anything I had ever known. I remember at one point feeling myself swirling outside of my body, not detached totally, but swirling around beyond my body, though still connected.

I forced my eyes open and turned on the light. Where was I? What was happening? Where was Pop-Pop? Where was I? As I calmed myself down, I began to think how inappropriate it was to feel fear. Pop-Pop was such a gentle, kind man who had loved me so much. I remember stories I had heard from my parents about Pop-Pop's strong feelings toward me. In one such story I had been hospitalized at age three to have my tonsils out. Apparently Pop-Pop would sit in his car in front of the hospital for hours, looking up at my window during the time there were no visiting hours.

Once again I felt as if Pop-Pop was here watching. After some moments I turned off the light, closed my eyes, and actually did manage to slip into a light sleep for a few more hours. When the alarm clock went off, I showered, dressed, and began an active day of teaching mental health workers the different ways of dealing with stress in the workplace.

Some eight hours later, on a train heading back to Philadelphia, I finally had the time to think quietly about my experience. My mind shifted to my son, Philip, who had been named after Pop-Pop. Philip would be twenty years old in a few months. This was April, the month Pop-Pop had died. Did Pop-Pop come back in recognition of the twentieth anniversary of his death? Tears flowed down my face. I knew now that Pop-Pop was aware of his namesake. I will always cherish the feeling of love I experienced in that motel room in Fredericksburg.

Eleanor: Moving on

Eleanor was a friend of mine who had been diagnosed with a malignant melanoma. I remember the sadness I felt the first time I visited her at the hospital after her surgery. I sat with this brave young woman, who at the time was trying hard to convince herself that everything would be all right and that she would be back to work in a few weeks. Her husband, Jerrord, was helping his mother look after their two young children.

Eleanor came out of the hospital and worked very hard at putting this experience behind her. We had lunch together about once a month and discussed issues ranging from family concerns and women's rights to spirituality—and at times we focused on her fears that returned before each of her cancer checkups.

Several years later a checkup showed that the cancer had spread to her liver. Eleanor left work and grew weaker over a period of a year. During my visits, she always expressed concern for Jerrord and their children. She increasingly became agitated and depressed, and she avoided any acknowledgment of death. For several months I sensed that she did not want to see me, and I respected her wishes. One day Eleanor's mother called me at my office to say that Eleanor wanted to see me again. I went to the hospital that same day, only to find Eleanor looking very pale and ill. She cried quietly as she expressed her deep concern over how Jerrord and her children would cope when she died. I told her firmly, but gently, that I believed she was ready to pass on . . . that she should go in peace, trusting that her family would be all right. I further asked her if there was anything else she thought she could do to help them. She quietly replied "no" and then handed me several letters to give to Jerrord, her children, and her mother after she was gone. I whispered in her ear that it was time to let go. She smiled and hugged me and we each expressed how we loved each other. I said good-bye.

Two days later her mother called me to say that Eleanor had died, and that at the moment of death she suddenly looked up at the ceiling and with a big smile said, "Tell Judy that I saw the light."

About eight months later, Eleanor came to me as I slept. She appeared to be in a smoky mist as she expressed concern for her family's welfare. I conveyed to her through my thoughts that they were really doing fine and would be better in the months ahead. I then communicated what I had said to her before, when she was still alive: "Eleanor, it's time for you to let go. You must think of yourself now and move on." At that moment my alarm clock went off; startled, I awakened.

Two weeks later I saw Jerrord. He told me Eleanor had come to him in a dream, in a smoky mist, conveying her concern about his and the children's well-being. It turned out to be the same date that she had come to me. How meaningful it felt to know that I could communicate with Eleanor, even after she had died.

My Irish Water Spaniel

Another personal encounter with death involved my beloved pet of more than thirteen years, *Meatball*, an Irish water spaniel whom Marty and I had bought when we moved to our new home in the woods overlooking a creek. Through research we discovered that Irish water spaniels have webbed feet and enjoy frolicking in water. We then discovered that there was a breeder of such dogs in New England, and after seeing how cute they were, we made arrangements to meet our new puppy—after his air flight from

New Hampshire—in the baggage department of the Philadelphia airport.

As our eyes spotted the crate that held our dog, it was love at first sight for me. Irish water spaniels are distant cousins of the poodle, and as a result he was covered with tight chocolate-brown curls except for the top of his hairdo, where wild-looking wavy "bangs" fell over his golden eyes. How excited we all were that day. We even brought our other puppy, *Eggroll,* along for the ride. Eggroll was a wire-haired dachshund about eighteen months old. It was funny to see them together—the large, fuzzy, clown—like dog looking down at this small, dignified dachshund, who wasn't completely sure yet what to make of the new family member. Eggroll (named for the dachshund—like shape of the Chinese culinary delicacy) and Meatball (I'm still not sure why that name came to mind) became a loving, comical, wondrous pair.

The dogs kept each other company when we were out each day at work and school. When I changed my schedule and met with clients at home, Meatball would lie at my feet throughout the sessions. He was sensitive to my clients' emotions as well as to my responses. He waited respectfully until the session ended, then rose, and majestically escorted the client to the door.

For the last few years of his life, Meatball had trouble climbing stairs and running. The veterinarian said Meatball's rear leg muscles had degenerated. He followed me from room to room. Even at the beach, he walked quietly by my side. Occasionally, he chased a beach crab, then stopped suddenly, turned, and waited for me.

Thirteen and a half years from the day he arrived in our lives, Meatball passed away at the New Jersey shore. I was at a workshop in British Columbia the day he died. Marty buried him in the dunes by our beach home. Later, when I arrived home, I stood on the grave site thinking of that unforgettable dog and communicated with him in my mind. I told him to feel happy and secure wherever he was—and at that exact moment, under the dark night sky, a solitary beam of light moved rapidly across the grave and exploded in the blackness of the beach. This time, rather than tell myself it was a firefly or search for some other explanation, I just let myself feel gratitude.

One morning several weeks later, I awoke early, jumping out of bed with eyes half closed to turn off the alarm clock. I had deliberately placed the clock on a bureau half way across the room to ensure that I would get out of bed. As I headed back to bed for a few more moments of rest on that dark, rainy morning, I caught sight of Meatball lying in his usual position on the small rug next to my side of the bed. I buried my head in my pillow. When Marty asked me what was wrong, I told him, and we both looked on the rug, but Meatball was gone.

During my weekend excursions to the shore I decorated Meatball's grave. Marty had originally put a sturdy piece of wood at the site to serve as a marker. Around this I placed shells, pretty stones, twigs of trees, a feather inserted in the sand, and his feeding dish. Each time I visited the shore I was comforted in standing there admiring the treasures and feeling closely connected to our spaniel. Over the next few months two severe hurricanes struck the New Jersey shore, causing much beach erosion and property damage. After the second storm Marty drove to the shore to examine our home. He telephoned to tell me everything seemed okay except for the markers on Meatball's grave site—they had been swept away.

As I pulled into the driveway of our beach house, I spotted Meatball's weighted dish turned upside down about fifty feet from the dunes. And then, as I walked over the dunes to look for a clue to his grave site, I blinked in disbelief. There was the feather that months before I had gently pushed into the sand, still swaying slightly in the breeze. I joyfully reconstructed Meatball's grave site and redecorated it with more shells and stones placed around the feather. My dog and I were together, and miracles continued to define my everyday world.

For those of you who feel emotionally close and connected to your pets, be open to the fact that such a relationship is indeed profound. When an animal passes on, let your feelings of closeness guide you, and be open to your pet's attempts at loving communication.

UNDERSTANDING DEATH

Like near-death experiencers, I no longer fear death. Over the years my inner journey and explorations have moved me far beyond the death anxiety that I felt as a teenager. Through my direct connection, as well as through study, I know that death is not the end but rather represents a new beginning.

Belief in an afterlife is part of Christianity, but in our Western culture religion has not been integrated into our everyday life. Eastern cultures have held on more to spiritual traditions and philosophies in which death is not seen as the end of existence. Rather, consciousness in some form continues after biological death. Egyptian and Tibetan traditions provide detailed descriptions of the afterlife in terms of phases and sequences that an individual who has just died may encounter. Hindus and Buddhists see death as far superior to life and as representing a spiritual awakening.

An important concept in these traditions is the idea of reincarnation. Reincarnation is the process by which each soul lives many lives in order to purify itself. The manner in which one lives and learns the lessons in each particular lifetime, as well as the attitudes and knowledge a person demonstrates toward his or her own dying, will influence future incarnations.

From a psychological point of view, it is also my belief that the manner in which each of us will face our own death is strongly influenced by the ways that we confront the multiple challenges and problems in our everyday lives. For example, when we are able to confront the pain and fear related to a particular situation, and then move through the consequences and resulting losses or necessary changes, we are practicing what it feels like to die. Any change or loss, then, becomes a miniature death. And as we begin to engage in new behaviors, behaviors that come from letting go of old self-defeating thoughts and feelings, we begin to lose big parts of ourselves and experience a sense that we are dying.

At a psychospiritual level this is called an *ego death*, and our subsequent emotional liberation, or new way of being, becomes a *rebirth*. These ego deaths and rebirths prepare us for a life of higher functioning as well as for dealing with our ultimate physical annihilation.

Once we die, our individual souls move toward the next stage or level on our respective spiritual paths. These stages represent where we are on our own unique journeys into eternity. The factors that influence the route we take on our spiritual paths are clearly open to question. Such perspectives are addressed in numerous philosophical and spiritual theories that could easily fill many volumes. The place on our path at a given time is affected by such variables as the number and kinds of past incarnations we have had, our soul's purpose in a particular lifetime, and the choices, decisions, and lessons we have learned.

I no longer question survival after death. I encourage you to begin to acknowledge your own mortality at a deeper level. As you do this, you will find life opening up to you in new ways. You will discover that you can live life more fully in the present, with more intensity and with a greater sense of confidence and security. This new perspective will mark the beginning of a journey that can transform your life in ways that you never imagined.

PART II

A Foot in Two Worlds

Energy from higher realms can heal.

CHAPTER 4
A Priest and the Tree of Life

Psychic phenomena, paranormal phenomena, and spiritual experience encompass a wide range of events that lie outside the perceptions of our normal five senses and, therefore, are not explained in terms of present scientific laws. As my psychic experiences multiplied and grew in intensity, I found it difficult to ignore them. No longer could I direct my interests only toward the professional and academic world that I had regarded as so safe and familiar.

My typical sequence of events for integrating these experiences occurred in five steps: first, there was the experience; second, I repressed it; third, shortly thereafter I remembered it; fourth, I "magically" came upon a book or some other source of information that explained it; and fifth, I felt intellectually assured so that I could put the experience on some back shelf in my mind and get on with my life.

But one can cover things up only so much, and I finally reached a point where the repression became more and more difficult. Along with a growing sense that I was feeling split much of the time, with one foot in each of two worlds, I began to regard my professional work as not reflective of who I was. These feelings made no rational sense to me.

During this nine year period I worked for Matrix Research Institute, traveling around the country, lecturing and working with other mental health professionals who for the most part worked with serious mentally ill persons. At Matrix I felt close to my colleagues. In addition, I maintained a small private practice and taught at the college level. So what was wrong? Increasingly, I felt that in order for me to be who I was, I needed to make a change. I needed to incorporate my experiences of expanded consciousness into my work as a psychologist. At the same time, because of my ambivalence regarding these phenomena, I challenged my own thoughts and feelings, and often told myself how foolish I was being. How could I possibly be authentic as a psychologist when, in this part of the world in the 20th century, psychology relegated these experiences to the realm of psychopathology? I felt alone and confused.

Finally I consulted a well-respected psychiatrist. The choice to consult a traditional therapist clearly paralleled the conflict I felt regarding what was happening to me. We developed a good relationship, and I felt hopeful that he would help me work out my job-related problems, and also help me to understand and incorporate my "unusual experiences" that seemed so related to my professional dilemma. His focus, however, quickly centered on early issues related to feelings that I had about my parents. When I brought up my "experiences," he invariably grew uncomfortable, began to pace around his office, and stated, "I don't deal with my creative patients' creativity." Although he was honest, I felt frustrated and misunderstood. I finally ended our therapeutic relationship, again feeling very much alone.

BREATH WORKSHOPS—
EXPANDED CONSCIOUSNESS

Within a week after I had terminated work with the psychiatrist I received a newsletter from a psychological association to which I belonged, and in it was announced a three-year intensive program in consciousness studies for mental health professionals led by Dr. Stanislav Grof, a psychiatrist from Czechoslovakia and researcher in human consciousness. This opportunity could not have come at a better time.

At first I was excited about the prospect of participating, then nervous. I had read some of Dr. Grof's books and knew that he worked with the deepest parts of the psyche, inducing altered states through breathing and music. After some resistance, I followed their protocol and wrote a description of my life and many unusual experiences, explaining why I wanted to engage in this work, and included my resumé. After I mailed the application, I put the matter out of my mind. About a month later I was accepted into Dr. Grof's program.

As my van drove up the long, unpaved, winding road to the workshop center, surrounded by the rolling hills and grapevines of Northern California, I entered another world—a world far from the people, places, and things that so filled my life. How distant Philadelphia was, and how quietly excited I felt to have this opportunity. When the van finally stopped, the other participants and I arrived in a beautiful rustic setting where each of us was taken to our own wooden cabin that was to be our home. Then we all headed for the bright dining hall, where the rest of our group was already seated.

Twenty-six fellow participants were seated around large, round tables serving family-style vegetarian food. Everyone seemed open, friendly, and interesting. In the middle of this group was a large, dark-haired man, with brown eyes, in a plaid shirt and khakis, who came over to warmly say hello to the new group that had come in. He had a peaceful demeanor that reflected both a strong presence and a quiet shyness. He seemed to know everyone in the room but me. "Hello," he said, looking directly at me as he extended his hand, "I'm Stan Grof."

After dinner that first night, we moved to a lodge that I learned would be the setting for our work. It was a large, informal, square room, and everyone sat on pillows in a relaxed fashion. During this first session we made self-introductions. The group was divided about equally between men and women, and while the majority of participants were in their forties, the age span ranged from twenty-seven to seventy. Most were psychologists, psychiatrists, or social workers, but there were also some business people as well as a physicist and an environmentalist, among others. Whatever their vocation, they all seemed familiar with Stan's work and had engaged in various spiritual practices extensively on their own. Ken, a gentle man who wore Indian jewelry, explained that he had been working closely with a Native American shaman for many years. Clearly, this was a knowledgeable, spiritually oriented group, and the warmth and authenticity that everyone conveyed made me feel as if I had finally "come home."

The next day Stan began by discussing some basic concepts of Holotropic Breathwork. This is a method he and his wife, Christina, developed. While working with people who were meditating and using yoga breathing patterns, they incorporated music and discovered that through this process people were able to expand their consciousness more quickly and access some very deep parts of their psyches. He further explained that the breathing process usually lasts about two hours. The person who is doing the breathing lies down with closed eyes and breathes more deeply and more rapidly than normal while music incorporating ethnic, primitive, and inspirational themes is played continuously.

Half the people in the group did the breathing at one time, while the other half served as sitters. As one person breathed, the sitter watched closely to protect the breather's space. After several hours the breather attempted to concretize the experience through a type of drawing called a mandala. Then, after a break, the roles were reversed.

It is important to note that this breathing process is not new or unique. Many cultures have used it for thousands of years to establish a connection with God. From a more psychological perspective, it can be described as opening one's self to the deepest and wisest parts. Prolonged concentration on the breath can enable a person to expand his or her consciousness and move into an altered state. The music incorporated into this work has also been used in various cultures and throughout history. Primitive sticks, rattles, and drums, as well as more contemporary inspirational and religious chants, have for centuries played a role in religious practice, both within the church and outside it.

Energy blocked during the life process must be converted into freely flowing emotions. When a breather becomes aware of the places in his or her body where energy is blocked, facilitators utilize body work to help release this energy.

Breathwork may lead to a variety of experiences. These may include unresolved psychological issues and actual experiences that were lived through during one's birth. In addition, archetypal, spiritual, mystical, or paranormal experiences that go beyond the personal and transcend our conception of linear time and three-dimensional space may occur during breathwork. The latter group of experiences are called transpersonal. It is through such transpersonal experiences that we receive information from the universe.

Transpersonal experiences were encountered spontaneously through most of my life. These I had researched, read about, and then ignored so that I could get on with the activities of living. The notion of deliberately bringing them about was frightening. Would I lose control when I breathed? Would whatever came through the breathwork overwhelm me? Would I become psychotic? Would I survive?

The First Breathwork Session

After the first morning's lecture we were asked to pick a partner for our first breathing session. With this partner we would perform the complementary roles of breather and sitter. I was paired with a young man named Haru who had recently come from Japan to attend graduate school in the United States. His English was limited and he seemed quite shy. At first I felt uncomfortable, thinking that Haru and I would have little in common. However, after we had worked together and had gotten to know each other, we decided that we wanted to do our breathwork together for the entire ten days, a practice that is not ordinarily followed. The caring and respect that Haru and I developed for each other went beyond anything I had ever felt so quickly before. Our mutual feelings were unconditional and allowed me to appreciate fully how all people are really united in a manner that eliminates the concept of separateness or external differences.

I told Haru I was nervous. He said, "You breathe first, and then you will be better." So I did. As the deep pulsating melody began, accompanied by drums and other percussion instruments, I slowly descended to a state in which my mind shut down. In the beginning I felt calm, then abruptly I became upset and moved into a fetal position as if in the womb. I was aware at that time that I wanted to be comforted by Haru, but in my altered state, with eyes closed, I could not find him. It felt as though he was not there. So I held myself and felt secure in this position. I alternated between holding myself and lying on the mat with my arms and legs stretched out, feeling open, free, and somehow connected to the cosmos.

At one point I became a tree, with my legs together representing the trunk, and my arms spread out reaching up to God. Stan said this tree made him think of the Tree of Life, represented in the branch of Jewish mysticism known as the Kaballah. At another point I had a vision of a Russian Orthodox priest in black ecclesiastical vestments and miter; I brought my hands together, prayed, and bowed my head, over and over.

Throughout the experience, I wondered how I could be in a trance if I was aware of my existence in the room. Two hours later I opened my eyes. Haru brought me a blank white drawing paper with a large, lightly drawn circle placed in the center of the sheet. This was what was called a mandala, and it represents an art form that symbolizes wholeness. I was intent on drawing the images that were part of my breathing session. I did not want to be limited to the confines of the circle on the paper.

As I studied my mandala and sipped the hot tea that Haru brought me, I interpreted the embryo, the tree of life, and the priest as all connected to God, and I felt a part of all of this. It was a wonderful feeling! What was strange, however, was that I, an agnostic, was relating my feelings to God and spirituality. My images were linked to Catholicism and Judaism.

A conceptual framework for my spiritual journey has been essential. My deepest intuitive learning has come through direct mystical experiences. Through private study and through Dr. Grof's program, I was also able to develop an intellectual framework. I have always been motivated to investigate the deep questions of reality not usually addressed in our culture. My experiences have crossed cultures, historical time periods, and conventional ways of perceiving time and space. Each category of experience was borne of a previous one, and these in turn have then led to more expansive ones.

The music of my inner world has become so exquisitely refined and integrated that it would feel harsh and contrived to try to separate the melodic line into measures that pertain to a linear sense of time.

Awakening on Yom Kippur Eve

I learned of *kundalini awakening* at one of the earliest breath workshops. From the training program I came to understand that what is called a kundalini awakening was related to the energy experiences I was having. Kundalini, a Sanskrit term, is said to be energy of the universe that is feminine in nature. It was first identified in India several thousand years ago and is traditionally symbolized in Hindu, Vedic, and Tantric texts as a sleeping serpent coiled around the base of the human spine. When I experienced being a snake, Haru had to hold me back from moving into people around me who were also doing the breathing work. A feeling of excitement came over me as I writhed and twisted like a serpent, very low to the ground. Then I became a bird that evolved from the snake-and flew off.

This imagery continued in other breathwork sessions. Sometimes I became so active that I would begin to cry. At times I felt as if the energy coming through me was uncontrollable. As the energy moved rapidly up and down my spine, it eventually exploded into colors and various images. Several years earlier I had first become aware of seeing the color violet behind my closed eyes; now, during one early breathwork experience the familiar violet color appeared. It suddenly dissolved into a radiating white light. As this light bathed me in its warmth, I felt as if rain were beating down on me, like a plant with a small flowering bud in its center, reaching up to receive this rain. Then I saw images of fish—many fish, small ones, large ones, a whale—as well as masks that looked Native American. I also felt great love for my family and friends, as I saw images of some who were alive and some who had died. And when I saw skulls, I felt no fear but experienced a deep love, a feeling of being connected, and peace with all.

After this breathing session ended I returned to my room early and fell asleep for a short while. When I awakened, behind closed eyes I saw a beam of white light and then a cascade of eyes. The eyes moved down the band of light and gave me the impression of a waterfall. Sparkling colors flashed before my eyes—colors different from what I was used to visualizing—gold, orange, chartreuse. They were so spectacular that I called out, "Wow!" This vision continued for some time, then changed to what appeared as a woodcut against a background of black. From this background came many more eyes for several hours. Then they faded away.

This vision occurred on Yom Kippur Eve, the holiest night of the year in the Jewish religion. I later discovered that this cascade of eyes flowing down the beam of light is mentioned in the book of Genesis.

The concept of kundalini is not limited to Indian literature. It has been described in the ancient records of Tibet, Egypt, Sumer, China, Greece and in other cultures and traditions, including early Judaism and Christianity. The Pharaoh's headdress, the feathered serpent of Mexico and South America, the serpent in the Garden of Eden—these are all representative of kundalini.

KUNDALINI UPHEAVAL

Upon returning home after this ten-day breathwork session I did further study and learned that when kundalini energy is in its dormant form, as it is with most people, it is coiled as a serpent three and one-half times at the base of the spine. When it is awakened, it moves up through the system, through what are called the seven *chakras*. The chakras are described in Hindu and Yogic literature as subtle centers of consciousness situated within the spinal system. The lowest center is at the base of the spine, the highest at the top of the skull. As one awakens to kundalini energy, a type of spiritual cleansing may occur. The vital life energy becomes released, and, as it passes through each of the seven chakras, much inner and outer turbulence may occur.

People who experience this cleansing find their worlds turning upside down. If the energy becomes blocked in a particular chakra, much psychological and/or physical distress can occur. A person with unresolved emotional issues must acknowledge and deal with those issues. This energy can reveal the true identity of the individual and, in so doing, connect him or her to universal knowledge. This energy of cosmic consciousness, also identified as sexual energy or life energy, is considered both physical and psychic in nature. In India this energy is called prana. In the first half of a person's life, prana is expended outward in orgasm and conception; in the second half of life, the prana can be stimulated by meditation to be drawn inward and upward into the brain through the spinal column. In this second form it is seen as representing the evolutionary development and transformation of human beings in the future.

Prana has also been described as the primal cosmic energy that lies outside the electromagnetic spectrum and physical forces known to established Western science. Other traditions have identified a life force from which other energies and paranormal phenomena are derived—a life force that is parallel to kundalini. Traditional Chinese medicine calls it xi (or "chi"), the Greeks wrote of "ether," Christianity terms it the "Holy Spirit," and Russian psychic researchers call it "bioplasm."

Kundalini offered me exciting possibilities. I was struck by how these descriptions of a kundalini awakening paralleled my own experiences. At times, I have to acknowledge, my ego became inflated and I felt special. But more often than not those feelings of self-aggrandizement were closely followed by confusion and anxiety. It should be emphasized that an important by-product of a kundalini awakening is the psychological upheaval that one experiences as this energy moves and bounds up against the chakras.

As questions relating to my patterns of life arose for me—specifically, my work, relationships with others, and my professional goals—I had no idea who I was anymore. To whom could I express these feelings? No one would understand. I felt very much alone.

Ego Death

The term *ego death* aptly describes what I experienced during this period of my life. An ego death is the loss of one's identity, a feeling of alienation, and the sense one has actually died. The future is unfamiliar and seems out of one's control. This is not a very tranquil experience. How, I wondered, could I be feeling this way—especially since my day-to-day life appeared on the surface to be under control? I still lived happily with my husband and children in our home.

But as one moves through a transformational process, it is the inner experience that can cause such upheaval. The external events or relationships that are jeopardized as one undergoes an ego death are usually those areas in one's life that precipitate self-defeating or inauthentic behavior. As my kundalini experiences deepened and continued to manifest themselves as rushes of energy that streamed through me with inner colors and lights and general agitation, I began to grow more absorbed in myself. Now, when these unusual experiences occurred to me at home, in my "real" life, their effect and my reactions were considerably heightened.

It is one thing to feel currents of energy during a structured breathwork experience, in an isolated nurturing environment where this kind of event is part of the norm and where a teacher is there to affirm what is happening. It is quite another to experience such currents of energy while at the podium presenting a professional paper. None of my colleagues knew what kundalini meant. These times felt very frightening and lonely for me.

During this period of time I left my job at Matrix Research Institute and also my teaching job at Antioch University. This was the first time in my adult life that I just stopped what I had been doing and came home without any clue as to my professional goals. I knew I could no longer do the work I had been doing. I believed that my work as a psychologist should incorporate my newly expanding world. But how?

I began to see a few clients in my living room. At the same time I confronted numerous people in my life who I now realized were operating on different wavelengths. I spoke up for myself more. I began to feel more detached from people and experiences that had earlier played an important role in my life.

Around this time one breathwork experience paralleled what was happening in my life. During a workshop I found myself lying in an Egyptian coffin called a sarcophagus. As I pictured myself lying in it with my hands in a crossed position over my chest, I became aware of great peace. I felt comfortable in this state, which I perceived as death, and I felt no fear. After several hours I became dizzy and imagined myself rising out of my body, only to transform into a baby being born again. I was upset about leaving the tranquil state. Later I realized that this experience of my death was probably justified because of the turmoil I had undergone during the previous year—I had left my jobs and made difficult decisions about relationships and my professional identity. How amazing it was that by going deeply within I could access historical information that was so relevant to me in my psychological development, my everyday life.

I had undergone an ego death in the world, and now this ego death and rebirth became apparent to me in my vision. Symbolic death of this kind, re-experienced in such a deep way, not only provides a realization of the impermanence of biological existence, but also facilitates a spiritual opening and insight into the transcendent nature of human consciousness.

The cycle of death and rebirth was a strong component in the religion of ancient Egyptian peoples. In much of the mythology of Egypt and of other cultures, we find emphasis on the symbolic crossing from the realm of the living to the realm of the dead, or vice versa.

At this stage of my process I believed that everything I experienced was related to my kundalini awakening. How could I have known that my journey was just beginning and would take me in so many other directions?

Essential reality provides the opportunity to see the past, present, and future at any given moment in time.

CHAPTER 5
Shamanism and Spiritual Initiation

Another of the topics discussed in Dr. Grof's program was Shamanism. The word *shaman* comes from a word meaning he or she who knows. Shamanism is the world's oldest religion, thought to be 60,000 years old, and has been practiced throughout the world. In many cultures the Shamanic state is still highly honored. The Shamanic state of consciousness is a special or nonordinary state of consciousness that can transform and heal. It is even thought to be a type of energy that can change the weather.

Divine Wind

As I listened to this information coming from Stan, my mind wandered to the New Jersey shore, to a summer home Marty and I were renting. It was an August day, sunny, sultry and hot. That afternoon I had received news about my mother that had a very strong, unsettling effect on me. She and I had a complex, sometimes difficult relationship. During a phone call from my brother, I learned of her desire to move to Philadelphia from Florida, where she had been living for over twelve years. When I heard this, I knew that I was to face a major emotional challenge. Suddenly, the wind outside picked up speed to such a degree that windows blew shut and trash can lids flew through the air. I wondered how this could be—it was still sunny and hot. The strange weather continued and I didn't think much of it. Instead, I pondered my upcoming problems over my mother.

I was spending a few days by myself at the shore, and around 9:00 o'clock that evening, as I put the finishing touches on a professional paper I had been writing, a sudden dizziness, accompanied by nausea, came over me and the surrounding living room began to twirl before my eyes. I staggered to bed and turned off the lights. Once in bed, I heard the wind continue to roar outside the house beneath a star-filled sky. I dozed off, only to wake to an image of my mother. Deep within me I knew that something other than a meteorologic event was occurring. When the sun crept through my window the next day, the wind had stopped, the dizziness had gone, and although I felt weak, I decided to go to the beach.

As I watched the waves, I remembered the day that had followed my *epiphenomena* experience. I had stayed in bed to regain my strength, and then at 4:00 P.M. that Saturday I awakened feeling energized. I knew then that by 4:00 P.M. on this day—also a Saturday—I would feel better. I left the beach, went back to bed, and, at the anticipated afternoon hour, got up. "Of course," I thought, "I'm fine now," and then I stopped thinking about it and finished the paper I had been writing the night before.

Many months later, I felt awed when I read: "The visitation of

God is often experienced as a divine wind." There was a divine presence that came to me that night at the beach. It was there to prepare me for the upcoming difficult time when I had to decide, ultimately, to place my mother in a nursing home. Through all the problems that ensued during this period, I always felt guided and supported by a force beyond myself.

We also learned in the training program that a person could become a shaman in one of three ways: through inheritance; by becoming a disciple of someone; or through a Shamanic crisis, as manifested through a physical disease or a spiritual emergency. Further, in primitive cultures, a Shamanic initiate should not refuse the call—he or she can die if the call is refused. This was starting to feel very intense.

As potential shamans feel drawn to a new existence in nonordinary realms, they will often react with extreme psychological and physical trauma. This experience is called a *Shamanic crisis*. There are several ways of resolving this crisis constructively. One is to get help from someone who knows, another is to mobilize inner resources, and a third is to actually receive help from higher levels, such as spirits.

Stan also discussed how a potential shaman can be recognized by eyes that roll upward. My heart suddenly began to thump. Recently, many of my clients had been making comments about my eyes. They were saying that they noticed them moving up—particularly at times when I was working intensely with them.

As the lecture on Shamanism continued, I became aware that I was not feeling well physically. Waves of energy seemed to come over me, and I felt troubled by a great fatigue. I went back to my cabin and got under my covers in bed. As I closed my eyes, I saw tremendous lights. The lights seemed to come from the deepest part of myself.

A Vision of Owls

The next evening, two of the participants in our group led a Shamanic ritual. We all lay on our backs with our eyes closed and the lights dimmed. This was to be a drum and rattling session, and as we allowed ourselves to be lulled into the hypnotic sounds, we were told that each of us might become aware of our "power animal." A power animal, we were told, is a spirit in the form of an animal whose purpose is to guide and support us on our spiritual path and to help us feel personal strength. We were further told that we would be able to identify our power animal if an image of a particular animal appeared four or more times.

I listened to the exciting sounds of the drums and rattles and soon found my thoughts stopped. I felt energized by the sounds. Suddenly, from out of nowhere, an owl's head appeared as a vision. Then, images of another owl's head, a profile, then a large golden eye of an owl, and a flying owl, appeared many times.

When the ceremony ended, I walked alone to my cabin. I felt too overwhelmed to speak with anyone. I had grown accustomed to having my own private experiences at home, but now to have them affirmed and given a name seemed too much—so different from my world and life in Philadelphia. I quickly fell asleep and woke early the next morning while it was still dark. With my eyes closed, but in an awake state, I again saw more images of owls, especially their eyes. I grew aware of a sense of personal power and inner strength.

As I walked to breakfast, still feeling relatively shy about my visions of owls, a woman named Sharon came up to me. A member of our group, Sharon was interested in and knowledgeable about Shamanism. She said that while driving to this training workshop several days before, she found two large owl feathers on the road. At that time she felt that she should give one of them to a person at the workshop. She had gotten a strong feeling the night before that I was to be that person.

As I excitedly told her of my experience with the owls, she replied that the owl is an extremely potent power animal, considered an intermediary between the world of spirit and the world of matter, in that it carries messages from one world to another.

Bird Phase

Wondrous experiences continued, and then the ten days ended. When I returned home, Marty welcomed me with roses. I knew that he would be sensitive and respectful of my otherworldly pursuits, and at the same time he would help to keep me firmly grounded in this world. Whenever I returned home after these adventures, I was shaky and fragile at first, and needed a few days to return to normal. But this time was different. I discovered that I could no longer go back to feeling "normal." As I walked on the streets, in the fields, and on the beach in front of our summer home, I kept finding and picking up bones and feathers. I also began to awaken in the middle of the night and have visions, as I had in my breathwork sessions. In these visions I would often be buried in bones at the bottom of the earth. Sometimes I would close my eyes and see the friendly face of an owl who had begun to bring me feelings of warmth and joy.

About two weeks after I returned home, a strange process began to happen with about eight people with whom I was working. One woman, a prospective client, called me for the first time and said she had heard about me but had put off calling me until an event happened that she felt was especially significant. She said that she had been having a dream about me at the same time that a bird crashed into her window. I thought this was strange but gave it no more attention until the next day, when I was sitting with another client—I conduct my client work in my living room, a space that is very beautiful to me, sunny and filled with plants, paintings, and all my special treasures collected over the years. As we sat on the overstuffed sofa that looks out on the woods, a bird suddenly crashed into the large glass window and dropped to the ground.

Within that week, seven other clients told me stories of birds that crashed into their windows at home or into their cars! One client phoned to tell me that in his dream I was a large bird carrying him as I flew through the air. This "bird phase" culminated when Jane, a friend of mine from my breathwork group, visited me at my home for the first time. For some reason, I immediately led her to a small sculpture of a shaman who had a bird's mask on his head. At that moment Jane became visibly pale and shaken and needed a glass of water. When I asked what was wrong she said that the night before she had seen me in a dream, in this exact setting, with a bird's mask on my head—the same mask that I pointed to on this small replica of a shaman.

Weeks moved into months and my Shamanic experiences continued at home. I observed what happened to me and I hunted the bookstores for anything I could find on the topic of Shamanism. I also bought a symbol dictionary and discovered that birds have been regarded since ancient times as mediators between heaven and earth, and as embodiments of immaterial things. Summer ended, and the next breathing session would begin soon. Several weeks before one of these ten-day sessions, I always felt slightly unsettled and too busy to even think about going away for this period of time.

The Next Breathwork Session

Upon arriving at the next session, I felt excitement and anticipation. One morning, feeling well after my breakfast, I telephoned my father. My father said he had a pain in his right shoulder. I attributed this to his arthritis and thought that at age eighty he was certainly entitled to discuss his aches and pains.

After the call, I entered the breathing room to carry out my role as a sitter. For the next few hours as I sat on a large pillow watching my friend Bonnie breathing near me, I felt an excruciating pain in my right shoulder. This pain continued through the entire morning session. After several of my colleagues—who had expertise in body work—tried unsuccessfully to relieve this pain, Patricia, knowledgeable in Shamanism, asked if anything had happened before this pain occurred.

"Yes," I replied, "my father told me on the phone about the pain he was having in his right shoulder."

"Are you aware, Judith, that as people are becoming healers, they often take in people's pain until they learn how to protect themselves? And did you know that in the Shamanic tradition, the right side of your body is considered the father side?"

Several hours later it was my turn to do the breathwork. As the music began and my eyes closed, I was pulled into the dark underworld where I saw my owl and now an eagle, and then images of bones and snakes flashing before my eyes. From these images I twirled toward what seemed like a higher world—one of light. In the underworld I felt a calmness that contrasted with the terror of the upper world's dazzling light, the divine world that I did not yet understand. As the light flashed beneath my closed eyes, I once again wondered where I belonged.

Alchemy

In the training session that focused on the theme of alchemy, I learned that alchemy began in the fourth century B.C. in the Hellenistic culture of Alexandria in Egypt. Its major sources were Greek philosophy, Egyptian technology, and the mysticism of the Middle Eastern religions. Alchemists projected the human experience onto nature around them, making no distinction between themselves and nature. Alchemy also incorporated spiritual and psychological dimensions, whereby one could dispel the impurities of human nature so that ultimately true spirituality could be achieved. Alchemy has been identified as a religious science (or scientific religion) whose objective was the pursuit of nature's secrets as well as a spiritual quest for ultimate understanding.

During my first breathing session at this stage of the program, again I found myself comfortably in the underworld. Instinctively, I pulled the blanket over my head as the music started, and I experienced the depths of the inner core of Mother Earth, an experience that by now felt like "coming home," as if it were something I had always known but had recently forgotten. It was interesting that my breathing sessions started from where I had been six months earlier. My process appeared to have its own developmental framework, a mind of its own, that would continue in its own way, in its own time, no matter what I did or did not do in the six intervening months. In this underworld I again saw owls, eagles, bones, and strange new visions of a lion, a vessel, and an ancient man with a hat, images again appearing as if in a woodcut.

As the session continued and the images faded, I became aware of the screams and strong energy in the room. I was frightened, became sick, started to cough, cried, and then felt better. Stan told me that this experience was important. I was so open that I felt other people's pain and fear.

The next day Stan showed slides of some alchemical symbols. First the lion, and then the vessel that I had seen the day before in my breathing session, appeared on the screen. Later, during a coffee break, I expressed to Stan my anxiety over the images I saw on the slides. He looked at me steadily and said, "Judith, when are you going to change your world view? This is nothing new for you. Isn't it time to accept yourself and relax?"

"Oh," I thought, "Of course."

Later that day my friend and fellow breather, Sharon, brought me a book on alchemy. I opened it to a picture exactly matching the image of the ancient man visualized in my breathwork. The book identified him as St. Magnis, a healer.

A Spiritual Initiation

My second breathing session, which took place the next day, again began in the underworld. This time I felt truly frightened. What looked like a monster flashed before my eyes. It felt like pure evil, and more and more I felt as if I were being pulled down. I found myself screaming, and at once I felt that I was in Hell and was shocked to feel so secure and comfortable there.

Then, suddenly, I found myself floating in a smoky brown void. It was an incredible feeling of total safety, a feeling of connection to everything there was, and yet a sense of being separate. I still heard the others in the room, but somehow I felt outside their energy field, almost as if an invisible boundary separated me from everything else—and in this emptiness that I felt part of, it was everything and it was nothing. For what seemed a timeless period, I lay perfectly still in this void, believing there could be no higher ecstasy than this.

In an instant, without warning, my head jerked back, and with a jolting intensity I was forced up into a sitting position. As intense streams of energy, dazzling light, and what felt like electrical currents coursed through my head and body, I became completely engulfed, overcome and vibrating. I shook and trembled and became unable to think, except to wonder if I could survive much more of this ecstasy, this intensity—and then it was over.

This was a major spiritual initiation. No longer did I know who I was.

That evening, wearing a new pair of jeans and long, sparkling earrings, I visited a friend's cabin for a small party she was hosting for our group. I told jokes with the others, and as I reached for a chocolate chip cookie, I threw myself on the sofa and began to sob. "Who am I?" I cried. "Would Moses eat chocolate chip cookies, make jokes, or wear long dangling earrings? Of course not," I sobbed, feeling like a fraud, living a life of hypocrisy. Like Moses and the burning bush, I had had a sacred experience.

My friends supported my experience. Later that night, Sheelo, a colleague from Germany, came to tell me about people who go to India and meditate for twenty years to have an experience like mine, and nothing close to that ever happens to them. He looked at me with wonder as he asked how I could live such an ordinary life in the world with the intensity of my experiences. I said I didn't know. I was glad he was there with me, knowing he understood as others did not.

At the same time I couldn't help but think of the many people who report similar occurrences during their "psychoses." Most often, someone like Sheelo is not there for them. Rather, they are told that such experiences are not "real" and that they are mentally ill.

A New Judith

As I began my breathing session the next day, I felt light-headed. The music vibrated, and I again found myself in the underworld. Animals and birds appeared and talked to me in a way that was surprisingly comforting. Suddenly I became Satan himself. I felt tall, powerful, and very much unlike myself. I owned the underworld, and I felt great surges of energy moving through me. Is this what psychiatry calls "grandiosity"?

Next I became aware of wanting to rid myself of my arms and legs. I felt as if my skin were coming off. I experienced a sense of self-mutilation, pulling at my body and feeling myself becoming a skeleton. At some level of awareness, I knew I was pulling off my T-shirt. I needed to have my skin freed from anything that was on it. As I experienced what felt like my skeletal form, I had a passing thought that dismemberment was not really that bad.

My body filled out again and I evolved into a new Judith. I was becoming transformed. I wore a long, black velvet dress, and around my neck was a large, irregularly shaped amethyst crystal. I felt as if I had gone through another initiation, and I let out a piercing scream.

As I left the breathing room at the end of the session, I felt twenty feet tall and enormously powerful. Outdoors, I took a long walk and passed a little store that I had never seen before. As I stepped into the store, my eyes fell on the same irregularly shaped amethyst crystal which I had seen in my vision. Quickly I bought it. Four years later, I still wear it every day.

Upon returning home I went through a month of electrical crises. Three times my stereo amplifier and speakers stopped working as I passed by them. As I sat under a hairdryer, it also died. My telephone crackled numerous times until it clicked off. Repairmen tried to diagnose my appliances' failures and came up with no clue. I felt agitated, but knew intuitively that this would all settle down when my body adjusted to the shift in consciousness that had occurred at my last breathing session.

About three months later, in bed one night, I read Roger Walsh's book *The Spirit of Shamanism*. In it he discusses the three stages of a Shamanic initiation. The first is a visionary experience of journeying through the underworld. There the initiate is attacked by creatures, becomes dismembered, and ends up destroyed. This "ego death" is often accompanied by images of hell. The second stage involves ascending into the astral realm, where the initiate is often abducted by an eagle and then identifies with the divine light. Third, the shaman returns to the middle world, the community, where a transformation to healer, or seer, takes place. Now the shaman has the capacity to enter nonordinary states at will for the purpose of helping others. By transmitting his or her energy to other people, the shaman can also enable them to enter these expanded realms.

How fortunate I was to have experiences, support, and resources that expanded my world in such amazing ways. What is equally important is to trust oneself, in spite of detractors, and to believe that a benevolent, universal force is always present, always guiding our evolution.

*Beyond the five senses, there is no separation
between mind and matter.*

CHAPTER 6
Beyond Time and Space

Two further aspects of my journey, the collective unconscious and the phenomenon of synchronicity, played major roles in my learning.

COLLECTIVE UNCONSCIOUS

Carl Jung, the Swiss psychiatrist of the 20th century and a contemporary of Freud, coined the term "collective unconscious." According to Jung, the spirit of nature brings its force onto the human mind when the mind is open. In this way the world's truth enters human awareness. Jung saw this connection as the human mind's radical tie with the universe.

Jung's work evolved as he tried to understand the symbols and myths that emerged from his own unconscious as well as from his patients'. He collected mythology and writings from the Middle Ages, from the Gnostics, and from classical works of China, India, and Tibet. He studied the dreams and waking fantasies of his patients and traveled widely, including to Asia and Africa, to decipher myths and legends. Consistently he discovered that similar dreams, images, and symbols of different times and historical periods presented themselves to people around the world.

My journey within, and its effects on my outer life, illustrate how I found the universe opening to me when I made that contact. I have discovered that if I want to more fully understand reality, all I need to do is to look within, not outside of, myself. Much of the visions, symbols, and information that came to me from the collective unconscious occurred after Dr. Grof's program in breathwork and expanded consciousness had ended. Initially, I had been overwhelmed. However, the meanings of my visions began to come clear from books or other resources that, magically, appeared shortly after the experiences. This learning through books compensated for the fact that I had no person in my life during this time who was my teacher.

Visions at Home

I would like to briefly describe the nature of these visions. After I completed the breathwork, I found myself spontaneously awakening in the middle of the night. Although I did not meditate, I then moved into a trance state in which I was fully alert. In this state, which might last for several hours, I have seen colors, lights, images, symbols, characters of the alphabet, or numbers. Even though I am acutely aware of my environment in a trance, I never open my eyes prematurely—the lids seem to be almost glued shut.

The following few experiences occurred to me over a period of a month. During these trances I discovered that I accessed mythology from the collective unconscious that was related in historical time and continuity.

Once, during a vision I saw a jagged line that I later discovered symbolized lightning. Then in another trance about a week later, the word "Olympia" kept coming to me. My symbol dictionary noted that Olympia designated the mountain where the Gods of classical antiquity lived. In the symbol dictionary I then saw a pyramid that I later learned could also be identified as a "ziggurat," which meant the meeting place of deities and mortals. I also had a vision of being burned up by lightning. In mythology, one story brings together a number of the pieces of these images. In one account, lightning represented ancient sky Gods who came down from heaven to fertilize mortal women. Classical myth says that Semele, a mortalized form of a Goddess and the mother of Dionysus, was burned up by lightning from her god-lover Zeus.

One day as I rested with my eyes closed, I found myself thinking about a relative who had been treating me in an unkind manner. As I thought of confronting her, I became aware of a conflict I felt because of her advanced age and failing health. Slowly my thoughts dissolved and I found myself once again in a trance state. This time I saw bright golden light and clear images. There in the light I saw a flaming sword, flanked on either side by a Buddha and a Christian cross. In the next scene I saw a vision of an owl smiling warmly at me. A sword is a symbol of decision, separation into good and evil, and justice. The flaming sword that drove Adam and Eve out of paradise symbolized both power and justice.

My anger toward my difficult relative was justified. Because of the symbols I saw in my vision, I had no choice but to challenge her behavior. The flaming sword confirmed the wrong that she was doing to me, and the differing cross-cultural spiritual images from

Buddhism, Christianity, and Shamanism supported my premise. My inner conflict disappeared.

How shocking it is to realize that so many people who have similar experiences are labeled psychotic. Their visions and voices are called hallucinations and delusions; and instead of being helped by therapists to understand the unique meaning of their symbols, they are given heavy doses of medication to crush these experiences within them.

My own experiences with the collective unconscious began to influence my work with clients. I could no longer work with them as a mainstream psychologist. When I observe how the symbols and images that emerge from the collective unconscious bring my clients universal truths as well as information specific to them, I am impressed and also feel that the work we are doing together is being affirmed.

When one taps into the collective unconscious, one's life can drastically change. Two cases that illustrate this point involved my clients Harry and Louise.

Harry: Surviving the Fire

Harry called to tell me that as he was doing carpentry work at his home one afternoon over the weekend, he suddenly felt overwhelmed with exhaustion. As he lay on his bed for about an hour with closed eyes, he saw a salamander. He told me that this image felt very intense to him, and he asked me if I knew its meaning.

The salamander is known as the only animal that can survive fire. Fire symbolizes the ego death-rebirth process. This interpretation held much meaning for Harry. At the time he had been confronting a difficult marital problem, one that had roots in his childhood. While attempting to change long-term patterns with his wife, he felt he was being rocked at the deepest parts of himself. This interpretation was an affirmation that he was on the right track. Thus, the image of the salamander served to affirm the difficulties he was experiencing symbolized in the dying of the old parts of his self.

Louise: A Path Toward Healing

Louise, another client, was seriously ill with advanced cancer when I began to see her. As part of our work together, I encouraged her to make the time for gentle meditation, which involved closing her eyes, becoming very still, and clearing her mind of thoughts to contact the deep inner part of herself. At one of our sessions she reported that during a meditation she saw a disturbing image of a crab, one of a Christian cross, and then a picture of herself getting off a plane to meet her mother.

During a previous session Louise and I had spent time identifying the ways in which her mother had been emotionally abusive to her. Louise felt uncomfortable acknowledging these feelings and thoughts, especially during her struggle over whether she should visit her parents in Florida. This trip would not be easy for her, but she felt that she should take it anyway.

Since antiquity, the crab has had several cross-cultural meanings. It has stood for mother, and in Africa it often appears as a symbol of evil. In Christianity the crab is a symbol of resurrection because during its development it sheds its shell.

After Louise and I discussed various interpretations, she resolved to go to Florida. The images that had come to her from the collective unconscious provided her with the information she needed. As Louise came to terms with the negative aspects of her mother and how these aspects kept her blocked, she opened up both emotionally and spiritually. Two months after we started working together Louise's health continued to improve—she was walking around, going out, eating well, and planning her trip to Florida.

Jung's exploration of the collective unconscious enables us to recognize that when our minds are open, the world's truth becomes apparent. Later, his work took him to the next step of relating the inner psyche to the outer material world of matter.

SYNCHRONICITY

To understand synchronicity we must think of ourselves as fields of consciousness unlimited by causality and linearity. The world is seen as a process whereby everything is becoming, not being. A person is an organizing pattern with fixed boundaries. The 300-year-old Cartesian/Newtonian model of the universe, however—with which most of Western culture identifies—views ourselves as solid matter. It is a model embraced by our academic and medical disciplines. It is logical, deterministic, and based on cause and effect.

Entering an undifferentiated state of consciousness, such as a trance-like state, can very often feel like death. It can feel as if there is a back-and-forth battle between a world not bound by time or space and the world of matter and the body. Because these states of consciousness can feel frightening, people will try to resist acknowledging such experiences.

Jung clearly understood the ways in which synchronicity turns Western science's perception of cause and effect upside down. That is why he conferred with Albert Einstein and Wolfgang Pauli, another physicist, to try to conceptualize an interpretation of synchronicity. Pauli believed that synchronicity made it possible to begin a dialogue between physics and psychology that would be targeted toward understanding nature's secrets.

Synchronicity, very simply, can be defined as a strange, meaningful coincidence—involving some form of pattern—that is not related to cause and effect. A person experiencing synchronicities often feels as if one foot is in consensus reality and one is in another world. Thus, the material world merges with the deepest regions of the psyche or consciousness. Synchronicities can represent essential relationships between the mental and material aspects of the universe.

In synchronicity, different objects and events congregate together to form a pattern in space and time. Therefore, a universal intelligence brings a coherence on this plane and the other. This intelligence is orderly and is connected to human consciousness.

I have experienced startling and wondrous synchronicities that have pushed me to the point of acknowledging that life for me could no longer be what I had thought it was. My first experience of this kind occurred several years before my *epiphenomena* experience, when I had never heard of the word "synchronicity." Before I entered graduate school I was going through what I have already identified as my "artist's phase." After painting mostly for fun, I decided at one point to meet with an owner of a particular art gallery to see if he had any interest in displaying my work. This art gallery owner was named Joe, and his birthday turned out to be June 18, the same as mine. Unfortunately, our meeting did not work out; he rejected my work and I felt deflated and hurt. If all this weren't enough, my dog at the time, a dachshund named Avis, was killed a week before my visit with Joe. Avis apparently poisoned himself by getting into a neighbor's gardening materials.

About one year later, after not doing very much with my art, I met another gallery owner from New York whose name was also

Joe. We arranged a meeting, and much to my shock and horror a week before my appointment to meet with him, my new dog, a beautiful Irish setter puppy named Avis II, was killed by a car.

I remember the moment, as I sat on a train bound for New York, that I got a startling flash. As I walked into the gallery, I immediately asked Joe II the date of his birthday. He looked at me curiously and said June 18, then really seemed puzzled when I began to pace around his office. I found myself rapidly rambling on about how each of my dogs was killed a week before my respective meetings with these two Joes, and how their birthdays are on the same date as my birthday, and so forth.

In spite of this rather strange interaction, my meeting with the second Joe went well, I displayed my paintings off and on in his gallery for two years, and we became good friends.

On the return trip to Philadelphia that evening of our first meeting, I dozed on the train. In a hypnagogic state I saw an image of a large clock with its hands twirling backward, alongside an image of an old woman who wore her white hair pulled back in a bun. Suddenly, in "real life," a woman sat down next to me on the train. She looked exactly like the woman in my vision. With eyes full of wonder, I felt in that instant that I was waking up to a dream. I don't recall now how our conversation began, but soon I was discussing with her my experience with the two Joes and my dogs. Her response was that time and space operate very differently than most people think, and that I was going to be given another chance with the second art gallery to learn new lessons so I could work things out differently than I had before. "But what about my dogs?" I asked. After some silence, she gently responded that we don't always understand all the reasons for things happening as they do, but we learn to accept that there is always a larger picture.

The synchronicities continued and became more frequent. I

realized that the world was operating on principles totally different from anything that my culture and formal education had prepared me to meet.

Over the years, other synchronicities involving other people and animals have occurred. One that comes to mind involves Jeff, a client who is very connected to animals and was going through his own deep transformational process. One day I was driving with my brother in my neighborhood and we came upon a horrifying sight. A deer who had run across the road from the woods must have become frightened and run by mistake into an iron fence that surrounded a home. The deer had plunged into the iron point of the fence and was dying or already dead as we drove by. A man who had stopped at the scene told us to go on—it was too late to help the deer. That evening Jeff telephoned me to say that when he returned to his farm that afternoon, he found, to his horror, the head of a deer placed at the door of his house.

Symbolically, in the northern region of Eurasia the deer is an important lunar animal, which as a spirit guide is closely associated with night and the realm of the dead. Very often as one is going through an ego death-rebirth process, images as well as material manifestations of death will become prevalent.

I have found that people who are working closely with me seem to tap into an energy field whereby we will share similar experiences that represent a force which goes beyond time and space. An example of this involves an aviary that Marty had installed in our home. In it were four finches that were quite interesting-especially when they multiplied from four to thirteen after only a month. About two weeks after we got them, I opened the window of their home to feed them, and one little brown bird flew out. After I tried unsuccessfully to catch him, I locked the doors of the room in which he was flying, and I slept fitfully for the duration of the night. The next morning I had an 8:00 A.M. appointment with a client named Hilda, who, I knew, often went camping. Around 7:00 A.M. I called her to ask if she had a net that she could bring to the house. She answered the phone, but before I could pose my request she told me of a dream she had just had, wherein she saw the little brown bird that had escaped. Hilda brought a net, captured the bird, and later accepted two baby birds subsequently born to the bird she had saved.

One other synchronicity that may be of interest occurred after a breath workshop in which one of my visions had been of a large eye with rays coming from it. I later learned that in Christian art an eye surrounded by sun rays signifies God. Upon my return home, a friend presented me with a gift. Tanya had been to Morocco while I was at my workshop, and she brought me a tile of a large eye, which in the Muslim tradition represents Allah and omniscience. How thrilled I was to receive this gift! As I was experiencing this vision during my altered state in British Columbia, she had encountered the same symbolic image in another part of the world and somehow made the decision to bring it to me.

These synchronicities have occurred during periods of intense transformational change. It feels almost as if the energy within is so strong that it erupts into the external world with the force that is necessary to create and affect matter. Such occurrences in people's lives can bring incredible joy and security as they recognize the essential relationship between the mental and material aspects of the universe. Tragically, psychiatry diagnoses these experiences as "ideas of reference." Individuals who experience their own synchronicities should feel appreciative; the major message again is to trust one's own experience.

Synchronicities imply that the script is written and is operating in relation to a divine intelligence. Physics and mysticism are related. The mystic sees the unity of all things and the ways that one can transcend the individual self and find enlightenment. Many of my synchronicities have involved another person. I have increasingly become aware of a lack of separation between myself and others. As we tap into higher levels of consciousness—where there is no real separation between our respective energy fields—a unity and interconnectedness evolves that moves us each toward a divine center.

Carl Jung's interpretation of synchronicity enabled me to understand reality in ways that went beyond the five senses. As my spiritual development continued to evolve, my understanding of time and space expanded even further. I now know that everything that exists has a part in an overall, purposeful cosmic plan. God orchestrates all of this and represents the one ultimate truth.

FURTHER DIMENSIONS

The first time that I felt as if I were actually moving in space—in a manner that was more than three dimensional was during a vision. In this particular vision the sky appeared to be breaking up. I sensed that I was moving through clouds, going deeper into them, layer beyond layer. It felt exhilarating, as if the heavens were opening up to me. I actually experienced the movement and the quality of multiple dimensions as I entered the depths of the universe.

Later I read that as Jesus was being baptized by John, he had a similar vision. This vision, identified in Mark 1:10, was described in the following way: "He saw the heavens opened and the Spirit descending upon him like a dove."

A Scientific Perspective

Normally people see in two dimensions, which appear as height and width. When we watch television, see a movie, or have a dream, these two dimensions are what we perceive. Depth is the third dimension, and usually we need to touch or have physical contact with a particular object to perceive its depth. What I experienced in my vision of the heavens did not fit the commonly acknowledged five senses.

Paradoxically, the most advanced theories of science and mathematics have incorporated the mystical into their ways of thinking. Albert Einstein, for example, identified his general theory of relativity as being inextricably mixed with dream and vision. Einstein also saw space-time as a solid four-dimensional continuum. He suggested that it was not at all clear why time flows only one way. And there is no reason that one should be unable to move back and forth on the continuum to any point in space-time. This fourth dimension is a scientific explanation for mysticism, and in this fourth dimension the space of our mind is multidimensional. Today, increasingly, researchers are also recognizing the far-reaching effect of a recently begun global energy shift into the "fifth dimension." While I am certainly no physicist, these explanations—from a scientific point of view—have helped me to conceptualize at least one aspect of what I was experiencing.

A Special Anniversary

As I slept on a plane to France, I saw what seemed like many layers and depths of black space—three dimensions, four dimensions, maybe more. I became aware of feeling unsettled, slightly nauseous, and dizzy, yet my eyes remained tightly closed as I moved through this process for several hours. Finally, the jagged corners and the breaking up of this space merged and became a two-dimensional flat surface again. And as I began to feel calm, my eyes slowly opened.

On my first night in Paris, I again awoke in the middle of the night. Behind closed eyelids I saw the black space move again in a zig-zag pattern of multiple dimensions and depths. Suddenly I heard a popping noise in my ears, and in an instant the black shifting space became an extraordinary bright light. This light then became the background for various images. The first image I saw was a thick wooden cross. This cross, unlike the Christian cross, appeared as a plus sign. Amazingly, I could see it from three and sometimes four dimensions—almost as if I were holding it in my hands and seeing it from every angle at the same time. I later learned that this cross was a Greek cross that had been common before Christianity.

Following the image of the cross, I saw ancient Egyptian figures and motifs, then a finger, a navy-blue sleeve with gold embroidery that looked to me like it was part of a navy officer's uniform, and finally a withered hand that appeared to belong to an elderly woman.

The next day Marty and I went to the Louvre. There, our guide described the sculpture of a woman, "Winged Victory." She said it had been damaged in a sea battle, and then she pointed out an adjoining glass case that held a "finger," which apparently had broken off from the masterpiece and been found a hundred years after the original sculpture was discovered. My emotions whirled as I recognized the finger from my vision of the night before and quickly made a connection between the navy uniform I had also seen in my vision, and the information that our tour guide was sharing about the sculpture being damaged in a sea battle. As my thoughts raced, our tour group moved through the Egyptian wing—and, sure enough, there I saw the ancient Egyptian images and motifs that I had seen the night before in my vision.

That night in our hotel room, after falling asleep, I once again awoke in a trance state. This time I found myself in what appeared to be a small, ancient, grayish stone-enclosed area. I was aware that this physical surrounding did not at all seem like a vision. Rather, it felt as though I were actually there. The stones surrounded me so that I could see their rough texture close up. Again, this experience involved depth and four- and five-dimensional space, not like the pictures that one sees behind closed eyes. The trance seemed to last several hours, even though time is unclear during these altered states. I finally dozed off, and upon waking the next morning, felt wonder at the intensity of the experience. At the same time I wondered what these various spatial phenomena really meant and why they were happening.

In the morning, Marty and I decided to take a day trip to Chartres, the magnificent medieval church that we had never seen, but about which we had heard so much. Later, as we toured the spectacular monastery, I saw the same wooden Greek crosses that I had seen in my visions a few nights earlier. They were thick, as I had seen them previously, and were placed throughout the church next to various scenes that portrayed Christ's crucifixion.

Next to the church was a small crypt that was open to the public. As I bent over to walk through it, again I relived the experience from my vision of the night before. I saw the same grayish stones and felt enclosed in the same small space. Later, at the Museum of Modern Art, I saw a papier-mâché sculpture of the withered hand of an old woman whom I had seen in my vision the night before.

What was happening? My typical emotions of feeling

overwhelmed, bewildered, panicked, exhilarated, and awed once again took hold of me. These experiences provided me with information to make me aware that humans have more than five senses, and that perception of time and space through those senses is limited. My visions of space breaking up into many levels had been followed by precognitive images of objects that I was to see in museums and churches. Clearly the meaning of these phenomena was that time and space are also linked, and that a linear progression of past, present, and future is nonexistent. I began to understand that reality can be experienced only in the moment—and in this moment, everything can be present.

Into Other Realms

My experiences of crossing time and space continued. Several months after the Paris trip, one evening I found myself in a deep trance. I felt as if I had no body; as a result, I was the space. With my eyes closed, I could hear my breath and feel that I was nothing more than my breath. I had some moments of fear, but overall I felt exhilarated, having no boundaries, no body, but being part of everything. As I enjoyed this total feeling of liberation, I then became a being from another galaxy, another realm. In this form I filled up all of space, the entire universe. Thus, I went from nothing to everything—and then back again to the empty space, the void, where I felt part of all there is.

A few weeks later, I entered another trance state. The first vision I saw was that of the familiar black space breaking up. Then a beautiful blue light coming from a realm beyond the black space overcame me. This light dissolved, and from beyond it came a dazzling, blinding white light. After being bathed in this white light, I saw a clear yellow light present itself, and suddenly letters of the alphabet appeared, all intertwined, as if on a continuous chain. The numeral seven flashed, standing by itself.

I had the distinct feeling of layers beyond layers. My process keeps going deeper and deeper, leaving me with a feeling that reality comprises many dimensions and realms. And this knowledge becomes clear when one is able to experience these realms directly.

The conception of alphabet derives from the Greek. Vowels symbolize spirit, and consonants symbolize matter. The word *alphabet*, then, is understood to be a union of vowels and consonants, and is considered to be representative of both spirit and matter. As such, alphabet symbolizes the totality and perfection of the entire cosmos. Seven also is identified as a number of completion and fullness, and has been regarded as holy since antiquity.

My experiences reflect the connection between spirit and matter; they are holy experiences that I believe are being guided by God.

OTHER BEINGS

The next breathwork experiences involved what the media identifies as extraterrestrials (or ETs) and what psychiatry calls madness. These experiences were mystical and sacred to me.

The Spiral City

As I increased the rate of my breathing and closed my eyes, a darkness descended. I felt as if I should not be in my body; I did not feel at all connected to it. Suddenly, I was in what seemed like a mystical world where angels and goddesses and light and joy seemed to envelop me. As I lay content, basking in this glow, little could I have guessed the startling event that would soon transform my world even more than it had already been transformed.

In an instant I saw a brilliant flash of a body of water, one that was different from anything I had ever seen before. I cannot explain how it was so different—it just was. Then in the same brilliant light, another flash. This time I saw an incredible city of spiral buildings. These buildings seemed otherworldly, and they appeared to be made of white marble. While in some ways it seemed as if they were from antiquity, in other ways they seemed to belong to the distant future.

These visions had a profound effect on me. As I recall, the body of water and the cityscape, the images themselves, may not have been utterly remarkable. What was remarkable was the emotional effect they had on me. For those split seconds I felt as if I had been dropped on a different planet, as if I were as far away from my world as I could be. These experiences were brand new to me and different from anything I ever knew or could have imagined. Excitement surged through me as if I would explode and then dissolve into nothing.

The cityscape disappeared, and a brown face with a large forehead appeared immediately. Its smile was so warm and kind that I felt no fear, even when I realized that this was an extraterrestrial being. Then I felt as though there was a gentle patting on the right side of my stomach, and then a sharp stabbing in my left breast. My thoughts went to Marty, Philip, and Marjie. Thinking of them felt so comforting—I became aware of my love for them—I wanted to be with them in this world, not in another. I then experienced waves of strength and power. Slowly, I opened my eyes.

As I tried to draw the brown head with the kind smile, on my mandala, I burst into tears. I felt that I had been so far away—could I ever come back? I didn't want to be back. My world would never be the same.

Surrender

The next morning I settled into the breathing process in a state of calmness. As the sound of drums beat rhythmically and I felt myself become one with the driving vibration, I felt surprise at lying there in perfect quietness and stillness. Where had my long-term, energized responses to this Shamanic rhythm gone? A quick feeling of disconnection once again came over me. My Shamanic identification had always taken me to the depths of earthly connection—to the lower world, to my femininity, to the cosmic mother.

As I lay there motionless, my arms and legs were suddenly pulled up—into almost a fetal position. Then in an instant my arms and legs stretched apart. As I lay on my back, I sensed a powerlessness that I had never experienced before, a sensation that lasted until I was back in a fetal position, huddling and nurturing myself.

No sooner had I found myself feeling secure than I was once again on my back. This process continued for several hours; but as the time went on I began slowly to let go of my fear. As I accepted that I had no control, my anxiety dissipated. When I could finally surrender totally, I found the white light of divinity enveloping me and bathing me in what felt like an all-consuming embrace. And there I lay, having totally given up my control and surrendered.

The Meaning of Extraterrestrials

The next breathwork experience began with my feeling more relaxed and calm than I had been before. In a very short period of time I had three clear visions that presented themselves in a background of brilliantly bright light. First, there was the image of a human being dying in pain; second, an image of a skull representing death; and third, large slanted extraterrestrial eyes, suspended in the universe, that merged into and became one with my eyes. At this exact moment an incredible golden—white light flashed out of my eyes and expanded to envelop me in its glow.

I immediately understood that these three steps explained what the extraterrestrial connection is about on our planet earth. Such mystical experiences provide knowledge through symbolic representation. The first image was symbolized by a person dying in pain, one who is going through a transformational process and, as such, experiences the discomfort that comes with loss of part of the ego, loss of old parts of himself that are no longer productive. Second, we have the skull symbolizing the total ego death of the person, the giving up of the illusion of the material world. Third, the person has now ascended to a level of consciousness where direct connection or merging can be made with other beings. And since the extraterrestrial is a more evolved being when this occurs, the contactee is catapulted onto higher levels of spiritual consciousness.

As this knowledge coursed through me, my body became extremely hot. I later discovered that the Ouichel Indians had the same interpretation regarding the meaning of extraterrestrial contact. Much of the reported stories of contact with extraterrestrials is sensationalized in the media. Reports are prevalent, reactions are fear based, and people who report such experiences are considered crazy. Many thousands of highly functioning persons have reported physical abduction and have manifested physiologic signs to support such occurrences. Others experience contact through consciousness. I believe that these phenomena are representative of extremely complex truths that cannot be totally understood, but are purposeful and need to be trusted.

The months that followed included numerous visions wherein extraterrestrial eyes appeared and were accompanied by Christian crosses. I believe that the extraterrestrial is a highly developed entity who can be in material or nonmaterial form and who participates in a cosmic plan aimed toward bringing human beings to more evolved levels. Through these encounters I have learned to trust, to let go of my fears (no matter how strong), and to know that when I give up my need to control, I will be protected. If one can face one's deepest fears and move through them, then darkness will turn into light.

PART III
Our True Nature

In addition to an ultimate force, there are many levels of energy, many realms and dimensions beyond the earth plane.

CHAPTER 7
Identity Crisis: Christian Mysticism

After Marty and I married we did not find, or seek, meaning in any particular organized religion. However, the birth and growth of our children brought me closer to believing that certainly there was some kind of God. My experiences of expanded consciousness also guided me toward the idea that a higher cosmic intelligence did exist, whatever we might call it and however we might explain it. While often overwhelming, these experiences could, nonetheless, fit into the theoretical base of transpersonal psychology.

With personal study and psychological exploration I felt that I was able to accept these experiences and still go on living my life in basically the same manner as before with my family and friends. But, as my experiences became mystical in nature, the ones which most shook my sense of myself were those that involved Christianity. Indeed, my sense of myself now began to change radically. My recognition of my mystical nature thus marks the breaking-off point between my old life and the new. The mystical person is who I am today and who I will be tomorrow. This is also the part of my journey that has been most difficult to accept, the part that has caused me not only to see the world in a totally different way, but to assume an identity that is as foreign to my original sense of myself as anything I could ever have imagined.

STIGMATA

A significant event occurred that seems tied to my writing this book. It took me several months to get organized enough so that I could cut down on my clinical practice and college teaching to make the necessary time to write. A portion of my Thursdays and Fridays was set aside to do this.

One Friday as I sat quietly at my desk making notes about what I wanted to write, I glanced at my left hand, which was casually resting on the desk top. I suddenly noticed that the palm of my hand was filled with blood. It appeared as a circle, about the circumference of a plum, quite red and thick. Startled, I looked to see where this could have come from. I found nothing. I then went to the bathroom to wash my hand and thought of getting a bandage. But as I wiped off the blood I was amazed again to find no cut or abrasion of any kind. The palm of my hand was smooth.

Just then the telephone rang. It was my friend Carol; she and I often shared life experiences and perspectives related to living life in a manner that extends beyond the material world. Carol had called just to chat, and she began to discuss how she was feeling a bit unsettled that day, saying that it reminded her of a strange range of emotions that she had felt some twenty years earlier, when she had visualized a stigmata on her college roommate's hand after ingesting some marijuana. On hearing this, I was shocked. I had not mentioned my bleeding hand. As she spoke, it became clear to me that Carol had unknowingly become the messenger who enabled me to understand what had really occurred.

After several days I contacted a Catholic friend who recommended a book called *The Bleeding Mind* by Ian Wilson. I learned that scholarly investigations have found that Friday has been the day when saints and other holy persons living in the Middle Ages manifested their stigmata, which represented Christ's wounds. This occurrence corresponded to Good Friday of the Christian Holy Week, the day of the crucifixion of Jesus of Nazareth. The mysterious blood had appeared on my left hand on the Friday of Easter week in the Christian calendar. Again I was incredulous at this event, and I pushed my emotions down.

Several weeks later, as I continued to try to integrate this experience with my everyday life, I began to feel that there was a reason the stigmata occurred to me as I was beginning to think about writing the story of my spiritual journey: the stigmata represented a sign or a guidepost intended to encourage me to carry out this task.

THE NEXT WORKSHOP

Weeks became months, and this stigmata experience, like others, gently settled beneath my active conscious life. About four months later I prepared to attend my last official breathwork seminar. This session would complete the three-year program with Dr. Stan Grof.

At the final breathing seminar, lilting music filled my consciousness and bright colors danced in my visual field. I saw myself covered by a white canopy as I lay on a table high in the universe, surrounded by a starlit navy-blue sky. I wore a white bridal gown encrusted with fruit, berries, and jewels. Beyond this canopy I could see the brilliance of divine white light, and I was sure that the canopy would be there to protect me and keep me safe as long as I needed it. When I was no longer fearful, I would be able to enter the light.

Feeling protected allowed me to feel warm and loved. Any fears of ending the three years of work with Stan and my colleagues disappeared in a split second. In that moment the canopy lifted off the table on which I was lying, and the white light from above engulfed me in its glow. Then I saw a beautiful blue eye with long lashes, and I was filled with love. I felt not only like God's bride, but also like God's new baby. I also felt alone. Earlier, I had decided not to attend two other workshops that extended the basic three-year program; now I changed my mind.

Crucifixion

During the first breathing session I saw brilliant white light that seemed to explode in my head, and I felt myself being pulled onto a cross. I spent the rest of this session crucified on a cross-basking in this white light. I felt actual pain in the palms of each hand, as if there were nails in them. I also saw faint images of crosses lying on their sides. I later learned that the same cross that I had visualized in the breathwork experience—that looked like an X—was the symbol of St. Andrew.

During each of the six previous breathing seminars I had attended, Stan would always bring in a guest speaker who would spend time presenting some related theoretical material. Dr. Richard Tarnas, a Harvard-trained psychologist who had spent many years studying the location of the planets at the moment of birth of famous people throughout history, was the speaker at this seminar. Richard's work adapted ancient astrological principles to modern science and astronomy and related this information to major historical events.

After the first breathwork session, Richard offered to share astrological information that might prove useful in helping us to interpret and integrate our sessions. He would look at a drawing of our experience and relate it to our respective dates and times of birth. My mandala showed a scared-looking female with curly brown hair being crucified on a cross. He told me that the planetary transits on my chart at the time of the crucifixion that I had just experienced during my last breathwork session, were the same as those that occurred on the day that Christ was crucified in the year 36 A.D.

Late that evening I fell asleep quickly, but awoke in the middle of the night to a vision of the numeral 3 along with crosses and a hand. In Christianity, *three* stands for the Holy Trinity. God's intervention is often symbolized by a hand reaching down out of the clouds.

Several months later as I flipped the channels on the television remote control at our beach home, I paused to look at a Catholic TV station. A priest spoke of Christ being on the cross for three hours and in his tomb for three days. I switched off the channel and took a walk on the beach to clear my head.

Death and Resurrection

At the second breathwork session that followed my crucifixion, the music began and I screamed as I felt myself, against my will, being pulled back onto the cross. I was frightened and resisted it, but to no avail. What was different about this experience was that several times during this session I seemed to fall off the cross and move into a fetal position under the blanket. Then after a few minutes I would return to the cross, but in more expansive ways than during my first session.

My arms became very stiff and sore. The music became driving, and in an instant I was catapulted off the cross, choking as if I were dying. I sat up, felt myself twirling around, and felt fright and confusion. Then, once again behind closed eyes, I became engulfed in light. This light felt incredibly warm and peaceful; my arms and legs became loose and flexible. I no longer felt stiff and rigid as I had on the cross, but much more comfortable. I remember thinking I could now move freely in the world. Being off the cross felt light, fun, blessed. I then lay down to relax, and with my eyes closed, in the direct white light, I felt dizzy.

I got up and wanted to go outdoors. I told my sitter that I needed to be alone. As I began to walk directly to the water, I became aware of feeling very strange. Where was I? It seemed as if I had died on the cross and was no longer in the world as before. Had I, like Jesus, also been resurrected? Would I have to physically die? Could I no longer be in this world?

My anxiety rose as I walked to the water. I asked aloud, "What world am I in?" The calm waters of the Pacific Ocean changed into large, noisy waves. Bees appeared from nowhere and began to swarm around me, and then I saw three, four, five black spiders walking toward me. The spider had earlier represented death and rebirth for me. On further study I had discovered that the bee is a Christ symbol.

Usually water brings me serenity, but now I felt anxiety and fear.

After I slept, I entered another trance. First I saw what appeared to be eyes without pupils. To me they represented death. Many more eyes with pupils appeared in my visual field. This felt more comforting. Suddenly I saw a flash of what looked like granite material. It felt to me as if my process had moved to rock bottom. I was now at the ground of my being—the word *truth* came to me—this was my core being. Is this death? Is this God?

The Ground of My Soul

My third breathing session caused me to be very much aware of my body. It felt large to me, and I pictured it lying down—as it really was—and divided into layers on the mat, similar to multiple layers of granite in the ground. This imagery caused me to think of a chart of sedimentary rock in a geography textbook.

I pictured my body as a type of earthscape that became surrounded in violet and white light. The top layer comprised my parents, grandparents, brother, and other close friends and relatives who have been in my life for many years. In the layer beneath were Marty, Philip, and Marjorie and our remaining pet, the dachshund Eggroll. Beneath that was Meatball, our spaniel who had recently died. Under that layer were all the visions, other entities, and archetypes that had come to me during my life: the wise Indian shaman, the cave woman, the goddess—all aspects of my deepest feminine self. And then, beneath this layer—at the deepest level—once again the image of granite, the ground, that which had come to feel like God.

Christian Mysticism

My fourth and last breathing session followed, several days later. No sooner had I closed my eyes than I was bathed in white light. The light felt so strong, so powerful, that I felt I was losing my whole being, that it was dissolving into this light. This continued for several hours, for the entire session. It didn't stop for a minute, even when I tried to escape it by going under the blanket.

Why did I try to escape it? All I can say is that it felt like too much. The intensity of this light was so strong that I began to feel ill. I really felt as if I were dying. When Stan came over at the end of the session, I began to cry as I described what was happening. I told him I felt as if I would die. He looked at me deeply but didn't respond.

Shortly thereafter I was on a plane, once again going back to my real world—a world that had begun to blend into what I was starting to regard as the spiritual core of my being. Before I had left home to come to this seminar, I had tossed some books into my suitcase; now I reached for one of them as I began my trip home. The book I picked out was titled *God Within: The Mystical Tradition of Northern Europe* by Oliver Davies; I had not read any of it before. As I started to read this book on the plane, I discovered that the granite I had seen in my visions was identified in Christian mysticism as the "sacred ground of the soul." What I had intuitively felt to be the deepest core of my being was identified in this book as a mystical reference that had been known throughout the centuries.

THE FINAL WORKSHOP

I decided to attend one more workshop. Returning to the breathwork center, a lovely retreat located in the sprawling wine country of California, brought back to me the thought that this had been the place of the first transpersonal session over three and a half years earlier. How insecure I had felt then! Now, more than three years later, I was back for what would be my last time.

Several friends of mine from our original group were at this seminar; among them was Sharon. She and I had shared many Shamanic adventures together. As I saw her all dressed up in her beads and feathers, I felt generally disconnected—from her, from other people in the group, and even from Stan. They were looking at spirituality from a perspective that emphasized cross-cultural traditions, the collective unconscious, and new physics. And here I was, feeling somehow a strange, personal connection to Christ, to God. My friends, colleagues, and teacher all seemed to be elsewhere.

A Piercing of My Heart

As I began to breathe to the music during the first session, I felt unsettled. My body jerked sporadically to the various rhythms, and I suddenly jolted upward, coughing and choking. After this initial expression of energy I calmed down and engaged in quiet breathing, which continued for a while, and then I became aware of bluish violet light in my vision. This time, however, it was more than just a color that I saw in my visual field—the color formed into a large ball that kept growing and growing until it seemed to spread all over and then explode. Upon exploding it encased me. I became still, quiet, peaceful. At a particular moment I felt as if someone were gently blowing on my forehead.

Suddenly, I felt a sharp pain, as if a spear pierced through my heart and out my back. Slowly I became aware of a liquid warmth flowing through my entire body, filling me with a feeling that I still cannot adequately describe. It was warm, moving, gentle, sweet, everything. After I lay submerged for several hours in this bluish glow, I finally forced myself to open my eyes. The breathing session was coming to an end, and somehow I felt unworthy of letting myself experience any more of this. Stan came over at the end of the session. Unable to talk then, I asked him if we could meet the next morning at breakfast. I needed help in understanding what was happening to me.

Alone in my cabin, I saw the same blue light that I had experienced in my breathwork. I panicked; I felt I could not take it anymore. I went next door where several of my friends were talking and relaxing. Bill, my sitter, was there. I began to cry in front of six people. "Bill," I said, "I'm seeing the same blue light that I saw in the breathing session, only I'm seeing it with my eyes open." He quickly said that he would stay with me until I fell asleep.

As he sat beside my bed, I closed my eyes and continued to see the light and other images—owls, dying people, terror—rapidly flashed before my eyes. I finally fell asleep. When I awoke the next morning I once again saw the blue light and the images—when my eyes were open as well as when they were closed.

At breakfast I reviewed my experience of the day before. Stan said the blue light was very important. And as I tearfully told him of my "spiritual emergency," he calmly told me I was very strong. "Why do my clients seem to get catapulted on their own spiritual journeys that parallel my experiences?" I asked him.

He said that the guru Muktananda could make pancakes while thousands of his followers joined him in the levels of consciousness he accessed. He explained that people who were working closely with me could sometimes enter the levels of consciousness in which I was traveling and join me there. He also told how Muktananda effected many synchronicities among his disciples. Finally, he said that he and his wife, Christina, had to acknowledge that their teachers—Muktananda and Joseph Campbell—were now dead, leaving them to be their own teachers. He followed this by saying, "Just as you have to be your own teacher now, Judy."

Many months later, I learned that the autopsy of Teresa of Avila revealed a hole in her heart, showing where it had been pierced. Then I came upon this quotation from St. Teresa in a book called *Mysticism* by Evelyn Underhill:

> *I saw an angel close by me, on my left side, in bodily form . . . I saw in his hand a long spear of gold, and at the iron's point, there seemed to be a little fire. He appeared to me to be thrusting it at times into my heart, and to pierce my very entrails; when he drew it out, he seemed to draw them out also, and to leave me all on fire with a great love of God. The pain was so great that it made me moan; and yet so surpassing was the sweetness of this excessive pain that I could not wish to be rid of it. The soul is satisfied with nothing less than God. The pain is not bodily, but spiritual; though the body has its share in it, even a large one. It is a caressing of love so sweet which now takes place between the soul and God, that I pray God of His Goodness to make him experience it who may think that I am lying. (pages 292-93)*

A New Path

After my breakfast with Stan, I brought the book *Spirit of Shamanism* by Roger Walsh along with me on a walk. To reach my special place at the breathwork center, I hiked a mile through some semi-rugged paths and hills. The destination at my journey's end was a rushing stream far below the cliff on which I sat. Somewhat breathless from my jaunt through the woods, I felt great peace as I gazed down into sparkling water that reflected sunlight creeping through gently swaying branches of leaves. For a moment it was hard to distinguish whether I was the water or the water was me. Then I randomly opened the book:

> *For Christian Mystics this return is the final stage of the "spiritual marriage" with God-the stage of "fruitfulness of the soul." After the mystic has united with God in divine love, this spiritual marriage bears fruit for all humankind as the mystic reenters the world to heal and help. (page 31)*

The words that I had just read pertained to Walsh's thinking that the shaman and the mystic can be compared to each other as they each made the "Hero's Journey." This explained the vision that I had in my breathwork several months earlier-the session in which I had seen myself, in a white bridal gown embroidered with fruit, lying under a canopy on a platform high in the universe. The fruit on my dress signified that my spiritual journey was going to bear fruit in the world as I reentered it to heal and help, but in a new way. And the bridal gown represented a spiritual marriage. Opening randomly to this particular page felt like a miracle

I stood up to walk back to my cabin. As I looked down at the stream, I found myself once again engulfed in blue light, and I saw a Christian cross that was formed from the trees that hung over the stream far below. But as I then ventured forth, trying to find a path back to my cabin, amid the trees and bushes, I felt lost and confused. On first glance I saw a path that was level and easy to navigate. As I began to walk along it, I realized that this way was taking me away from my destination. Instead, I needed to make my own path, up the hill and through the trees. This was not going to be the easy path that was level and clear. I was tired . . . I was lost. I sat down on a tree stump with panic rising. I let myself acknowledge that I was not in control, and I gave up trying to find the correct path. As I did this, my eyes spotted another opening through the trees. Once I surrendered to my fear, a new path opened for me. I followed this path, which was certainly more difficult than the first one that was level. It was uphill and covered with branches and thorns, but I made my way home on it. I was being guided, and I knew I was not alone.

Dissolution

The next morning, upon waking, I found that every time I would close my eyes I would experience movement, shifting dimensions, a feeling that my head would burst, and dizziness. Also I had an awareness that I was engulfed in blue light. When I went to breakfast, I felt as if my eyes were glazed and my pupils constricted with fear. Surely, if I began to breathe and closed my eyes, I would die.

I went to Stan and told him that I would probably die if I closed my eyes to breathe. I felt sure that if I did that, my head would burst. He looked at me slowly and steadily, and calmly he said that it was important for me to do just that.

As I began to breathe, my fears eased. I was enveloped in white light, and I began instinctively to massage the top of my head so that it could absorb this light. At these times I felt very aware of the boundary of the top of my head and of the light coming into it. And then I experienced the top of my head dissolving . . . and I entered into and became the light.

As this process continued, I massaged the top of my head in an effort to prevent the light from bursting it open, and subsequently I felt as if I was becoming the light, dissolving into it without a body. At these times the boundary of my head seemed to disappear as I became the light. I had no fears about dying. All I wanted was to move further into this light, but no sooner would this happen than I would become aware of the boundary of the top of my head again. Back and forth this went on for several hours—from dissolving into the light, to becoming aware of the boundary at the top of my head, which separated me from total dissolution.

Can I be totally absorbed in the light and still remain alive? I did so this day. The message that I received from this profound experience was that my access to the light is to be used in the world—and that I will be able to let it in so that I can give it out.

When Stan came over, his eyes closed when I told him of my process. He responded, "Death is always gentle."

This was my last breathing session. I was on my own.

Essential reality provides the opportunity to see the past, present, and future at any given moment in time.

CHAPTER 8
Process That Never Ends

A mystical process never ends. There is always a part of me which feels that this new reality cannot go any further, but it does. I no longer have a foot in two worlds as I felt that I did through much of my journey. Now my heart and will are merged with another reality.

The mystical path has been a difficult one for me to travel. At times it has filled me with a sense of joy, peace, and well-being that is almost impossible to describe. At other times, however, I have felt very alone. I no longer engage in any meditative practice to keep things going. The process now moves at its own pace and continues as if it had a mind of its own.

CONNECTION WITH GOD

I receive three kinds of information: universal truths, prophetic information, and personal insights. This information enables me to better understand a world that is filled with mystery and wonder, and goes beyond what my imagination or fantasy could create. The following experience occurred to me a few months after my last breathwork session.

The Silver Ball

I awoke around 4:00 A.M., transfixed at the sight of a sparkling silver ball that appeared in my vision behind tightly closed eyes. I was mesmerized by it for several hours—the silver ball kept breaking up into beautiful mosaic designs and abstract shapes like those seen through a kaleidoscope. As the sparkling pieces swirled around, numerous silver crosses appeared. The joy that I felt that night was overwhelming.

I was awake during this vision. It felt as if God was there with me, as if I was surrounded with holiness. As the sparkling images seemed to envelop me, rushes of energy came through me. I was also aware of my lower back, an area in which I had experienced trouble for many years. I directed some of this energy toward my back and felt the stiffness and discomfort fade away.

As this experience diminished, I fell asleep and had a dream of my grandfather Pop-Pop, now deceased for twenty-two years. In this dream he and I were at the ocean, one of my favorite places to be. Water has always symbolized spirituality for me. At the ocean Pop-Pop gave me a box, and as I opened it a large spider came out. I felt upset in the dream. All my past experiences with spiders came back to me. Each time I have seen one, whether in the worldly or visionary sense, I have come to expect another upheaval in my process, another ego death and another new beginning.

Later, I wondered what God was. I could relate to various philosophical and spiritual interpretations—an all-encompassing force, the ultimate intelligence, a mystery. I was "too sophisticated" to think of God as an omnipotent father figure with a long white beard and a white robe. What did Jesus Christ mean to me?

These visions I had been having—especially the last one that felt so holy—seemed to be separate from me. Clearly they came from outside of myself, particularly the Christian symbolism and the crosses. How then could I reconcile much of the New Age and the Eastern mystical perspectives that referred to God as being within us? What did it all mean?

The Holy Fire

Several nights later I fell asleep with these questions very much on my mind. "Where was God," I thought as I drifted into sleep, "Inside, or outside?" Once again, around 4:00 A.M. I awoke to a very intense experience.

I had been having a dream that had to do with being in some kind of performance—that raised the issue of whether I was being authentic or inauthentic—and then suddenly I awoke and immediately entered a trance state where I found myself burning up in the middle of a raging fire. The intensity felt so great that I questioned whether I was in the fire or whether I was the fire. The fire enveloped me, consumed me. At the exact moment that this experience began, I felt a burning in my chest that remained with me for the duration of this trance.

Finally it ended, just faded out. As my eyes opened and I saw my familiar bedroom and Marty sleeping beside me, I felt afraid. I tried to think, but I could not. Then I closed my eyes and dozed off for a little while. Soon I awoke in another trance state—this time I actually felt a baby lying on my stomach, teething and crying. At the same time I visualized a skull and crossbones. This was clear: another death and rebirth. I felt exhausted. I closed my eyes and went to sleep.

Fire is considered by many people to be sacred, purifying, and renewing; its power to destroy is often interpreted as the means to rebirth. In the Bible, God or the Divine is sometimes symbolized by fire.

Later in Evelyn Underhill's *Mysticism*, I came upon a quotation by 14th-century English mystic Richard Rolle, who described his conversion and God's contact with him:

> *The heart truly turned into fire, gives feeling of burning love. I was forsooth marveled, as this burning burst up my soul, and of an unwonted solace; for in my ignorance of such healing abundance, oft have I groped my breast, seeing whether this burning were of any bodily cause outwardly. But when I knew that only it was kindled of ghostly cause inwardly, and this burning was naught of fleshly love or desire, in this I conceived it was the gift of my Maker.* (page 193)

Walter Hilton, another English mystic, commented on Rolle's words in his book *The Cloud of Unknowing*. Hilton remarked that

> *This burning heat is not merely a mental experience. In it we seem to have an unusual but not unique form of psychophysical parallelism: a bodily expression of the psychic*

travail and distress accompanying the "New Birth." (quoted in Underhill, page 194)

And Madeleine Seimer, a modern-day mystic who lived in the early 19th century, reported in *Convertie et Mystique* being "seized and possessed by an interior flame, for which nothing had prepared me; waves of fire succeeding one another for more than two hours." (quoted in Underhill, page 194)

While it was somewhat affirming to read that someone else had an experience that was similar to mine, I still wondered why I was having experiences that had been documented by Christian mystics.

At the time of my experience of the Holy Fire, I awoke some four hours later to find myself floating in violet light. Space and time function differently when one is in an altered state, and so I had no sense of linear time. When the violet light receded, I found myself catapulted into what felt like a higher realm. Here was a light that was golden in color and bright beyond description.

Then suddenly, in this light, various visions came flashing through with illuminated brilliance. First there was a man in a baseball uniform holding what appeared to be a bat but was really a large bone. And then, instantaneously, the scene changed and there were two people. A voice from within myself said that one was a man who was in charge of everything. His name was Mr. Doyle, and the other person was his assistant, Ms. Armageddon. I also heard audible voices at this moment, and I felt as if I were actually holding several objects in my hand. One object was a feather and the other a piece of sacred sculpture that I seemed to know was from India.

It is important here to convey the intensity of this experience. The brilliance of the light, the clarity and surrealism of the characters, the voices I heard, and the actual feelings of the objects in my hands—these thrust me beyond my normal five senses.

Later that day, when I happened to glance at a book entitled *Julian of Norwich*, I noticed that the author's name was Brandon Doyle. It was about a female Catholic saint. As I read the cover of this book, I noted that Julian was considered a mystic/prophet and was known for her teachings emphasizing "God within us." Here was the answer to my question of the night before, in which I had asked whether God was outside of myself or within. God, in fact, is within.

Despite all my previous astounding experiences, each time another one occurs I become equally amazed. Once again, I felt awe that Mr. Doyle, the man in my vision, had the same name as the translator of the written works of this Catholic mystic. I also recalled how in my vision, Mr. Doyle was in charge of everything and Ms. Armageddon was his assistant. Checking the dictionary for the meaning of Armageddon, I discovered that it means "a final and conclusive battle between the forces of good and evil." What does that mean? I then thought of the baseball player with a large bone for a bat, and my eyes came upon another book that I also had not read. It was called *The Dark Face of Reality* by Martin Israel. As I glanced through its contents, I saw a chapter entitled "Can These Bones Live?" The following paragraph caught my eye:

> *When the necessarily destructive role of evil in the development of human consciousness is accepted, we can live more at ease with it as part of the total cosmic situation. Only then can the transfiguring love of God flowing down to us be received in our soul. (page 139)*

How perfectly and creatively this knowledge was presented to me. Julian, the mystical prophet who taught about God within, and Mr. Doyle, the man in charge, could be understood as the ultimate source of perfection and truth conveying the wisdom of God within. And Ms. Armageddon, God's assistant, symbolized the necessary role of evil or darkness in the development of human consciousness.

Prophetic Vision

Several weeks later I learned that a friend and colleague was very concerned about a medical test that he was going to have to determine whether he had Lou Gehrig's disease. As we discussed the possibility of this dire degenerative disorder, named for the famous baseball player who died from it, my mind suddenly recalled my vision of the man in a baseball uniform holding what appeared to be a bat. At the time of my vision I was not aware of my friend's concern about this disease.

Two days later on my way to meet my friend for breakfast to celebrate the successful outcome of his tests, I stopped to mail a package at the post office. On display there were gifts being sold for the Christmas season. I noticed a jigsaw puzzle that bore the image of a commemorative postage stamp of Lou Gehrig. It looked like the baseball player in my vision. The only difference was that the bat in the puzzle was made of wood, not of bone. I bought the Lou Gehrig puzzle and gave it to my friend at breakfast in celebration of his healthy diagnosis.

Synchronicities and visions notwithstanding, I remained intent on maintaining my professional work and family lifestyle. At the same time, I felt very much alone in my process. I no longer had a teacher and I had no worldly reference base or understanding of how to interpret what was happening to me.

MY NEW SPIRITUAL GUIDE

Shortly after I began to have these intense mystical experiences, I was reading *Mysticism* by Evelyn Underhill. First published in 1911, her book is identified as the preeminent study in the nature and development of spiritual consciousness. In the foreword to its twelfth edition, Ira Progoff, internationally recognized scholar, writes:

> *You may not be aware of it, but this unpretentious volume you are holding in your hands is one of the "truly important" books in the English language. By what criteria do I judge a book to be "truly important"? A truly important book starts with a subject that seems nebulous but before it is through it has conveyed the nature of what is nebulous in a way that makes it clear and definite.*

The Mystic Way

Underhill describes mysticism as a definite state or form of life. She suggests that it is obtained neither from an intellectual realization of its delights nor from the most intense emotional longings. Though these must be present, they are not enough. Rather, mysticism is an ordered movement toward ever higher levels of reality, ever closer identification with the infinite. She also sees it as leading to a heightened and completed life which has been found to be a constant characteristic of human consciousness.

The Mystic Way is a process which specifies phases that persons pass through as they travel this path. Although there are individual differences, there are also constants that have been identified throughout history. This model, which I use in working with many of my clients as they travel a psychospiritual path, involves two aspects. First, the typical mystic seems to move between "states of pleasure" and "states of pain" (as shown in my range of emotional responses to various experiences). Second, a classification of five phases is used. Taken together, these two aspects constitute phases in a single process of growth involving the movement of a person's consciousness from lower to higher levels of reality.

The five phases are summarized as: the Awakening of the Self; Purgation, or Ego Death; Illumination; Dark Night of the Soul; and the goal of mystical life—Union. The first three phases make up the Illuminative Way; the last two make up the Unitive Way. The Mystic Way is a gradual and complete change in the equilibrium of the Self. My own progression through these phases has never been along a straight line. Rather, when I am in one phase—which can be many months or even years—some influences from other phases are always occurring at the same time. Later I will discuss in greater detail how the last two phases of the Mystic Way have manifested in my life. Now let us briefly review the sequence of phases:

1. The Awakening of the Self

The awakening phase is usually spontaneous and abrupt, and is often accompanied by feelings of joy and excitement. In my psychospiritual journey, this phase was initiated during my *epiphenomena experience*. There was no joy for me at that time; as I interpreted it through my Western, agnostic worldview, I felt fear and confusion instead of excitement

2. Purgation (Ego Death)

The phase of purgation, or ego death, occurs when the Self becomes more detached from sensory pleasures or worldly ego desires. The Self, as it becomes increasingly aware of higher consciousness, realizes by contrast its own imperfections and the illusions by which it lives. The Self attempts to eliminate all that is not truthful in one's life, engendering a state of pain and effort. This occurred in my development when I dropped my job of ten years, my professional identity, and my relationships with colleagues and friends. For several years prior to my leaving, I resisted the strong inner tug that was not so gently nudging me to leave. Although I did not understand it at the time, I was fighting against a deep part of me that knew I had to work with people in a new way, one that reflected my budding spiritual consciousness.

3. *Illumination*

After purgation, transcendental consciousness returns in a more enhanced, intense way. In the illumination phase the mystic experiences visions and other phenomena that represent a type of training to assist and educate the soul. Illumination combines with the two preceding states to form the "first mystic life," or Illuminative Way. This third stage brings with it an apprehension of the Absolute, a sense of the Divine presence, but not true union with it. The phase of illumination, overall, brings much joy, happiness, and excitement. Many of my experiences were illuminative in nature. Meditation, occurring in the breathwork, without question speeded up the entire process. But this phase did not last.

4. *Dark Night of the Soul*

Phase four is known as the Dark Night of the Soul. As its name suggests, it is considered to be the most difficult of all the phases. The Dark Night of the Soul is also known as the final and complete purification of the Self, and it is often identified as a "mystic death." The consciousness that had in Illumination basked in the glow of the Divine presence, now suffers an equally intense sense of the

Divine absence. This means that one must learn to dissociate the personal satisfaction of mystical vision from the reality of mystical life. Ego attachments to transcendental experience, just like ego attachments to worldly objects, must be surrendered. Mystics are prepared for the final goal of Union by losing their egos, their individual selves, and their will.

5. Union

Union is the goal of mystical growth. In this state the Divine presence is not merely enjoyed and perceived by the Self, as in Illumination, but becomes one with it. The Mystic Way leads to a gradual but complete change in the equilibrium of the Self. It is a change wherein the Self moves away from the unreal world of the senses in which it is normally immersed, first to observe and then to merge and unite itself with absolute Reality. As this merging occurs, the material and spiritual life of the mystic are no longer split. The Divine is brought into the world of the senses. Life is characterized by peaceful joy, enhanced power, intense certitude, and permanent establishment of life upon transcendent levels of reality. The state of Union and the preceding phase of the Dark Night of the Soul together make up the "second mystic life," or Unitive Way. The completed mystical life is called "the deified life."

It is not surprising to understand how people in our culture would be emotionally traumatized if they were spontaneously catapulted onto the levels of spiritual consciousness that I have described in this chapter. The term "religious ideation" could clearly be applied to my mystical experiences. One has to wonder why so many people with diagnoses of serious mental illness report similar spiritual experiences, in spite of having different religious backgrounds or being atheists.

Beyond time and space, we are one with the Divine.

CHAPTER 9
Unitive Experience

Despite Western culture's denial of direct spiritual experience, all mystical paths recognize human potential in the same way. This chapter examines the true nature of all human beings from the perspective of Eastern and Western mystical traditions. Why is it important to find the commonalties that underlie humanity's spiritual and mystical traditions? Doing so will help us to realize how the same understanding of human nature has existed in different cultures, among different peoples, and throughout different time periods. For me, these cross-cultural commonalties affirm that mystical information springing from the direct connection is real. But as most societies move away from mystical thought and experience, entire cultures are being lost and people are losing their hearts and souls.

TOWARD UNION

Moving into the second mystic life—the last two phases of mystic growth—has enabled me to understand the nature of human beings as described in both Western and Eastern mystical traditions. About a year ago, I awakened in the middle of the night and saw the familiar black unidimensional field break up into multiple dimensions. As I then waited expectantly for some profound vision to appear, I was stunned to see the black multidimensional field change instead into a mere flat black surface again, what one typically sees when one's eyes are closed.

For several months prior to this, my visionary experiences had begun to diminish in frequency and intensity. As I go back to that moment in the middle of the night, I remember clearly the emotional pain I felt in the split second when I realized that no vision would appear. I "knew" in some deep way that my glorious, symbolic pictures were over. Then one evening, before falling asleep, as I was thinking about a particular issue in my life, for old time's sake I asked the universe if it would give me the answer to my question. I felt resigned to the fact that nothing would happen. But when I awoke the next morning, I was startled to realize that the answer to my question had come to me in a dream. The answer that I received was not anything that I had considered on my own. The next night I again posed, tentatively, almost shyly, a question that was related to a subject of importance to me. Once again the answer came through vividly.

And so began a phase lasting several months, wherein all my questions were answered through my dreams. Sometimes I would not even have to ask a specific question. I could just think about something, and I would then dream about it in a way that turned out conceptually to be more correct. Often in my waking state I would suddenly become aware intuitively of a wisdom that was not part of my conscious mind.

With the passing of time, my feelings slowly began to change. I began to feel that the answers that I thought were coming from outside of myself were really coming from within. As a result, I began to believe that the truth for everything lay within myself. Whether in dreams or by intuition, I could access this truth from the core of my being. At this core was God—God no longer felt outside of myself. Rather, we were one; we were merged.

As these feelings began to sink in, I experienced a quiet confidence, a serenity, and a connection to everyone and everything. Separations and dualities dissolved. Everything was part of this universal consciousness, part of God. Personal problems and concerns no longer felt the same. It is difficult to describe the sensation of expansiveness that comes from feeling at one with God and the universe, knowing that we are much more than our bodies and egos. When we give up our egos and make room for the God energy to fill us, this makes us everything and nothing at the same time. Could there be anything more than this?

MERGING

Before much time passed, I discovered there was something more. One night I awoke in a trance in which I found myself in clear light. In the past, the breaking up of space had always been black; this time it was light. But this light appeared in a new way. It was without movement, and at the same time it presented itself geometrically with depth. I found myself watching this plain, clear light for many hours. It seemed filled with everything, even though I saw no images or symbolic representations.

As I became mesmerized by this clear light, I heard a musical rhythm, a rhythm that remained constant, that sounded like music I would expect to hear at a circus. This experience was happy, transparent, wondrous, as if I were under a big top. And then I had the feeling that I was lying on the ground, at the very bottom of the big top. I saw an opening at the top of what appeared to be a semi-arched, immense expanse of light. I knew in a very deep way that there were many places to go beyond this expanse of light.

Suddenly, through this opening, I saw beams of light coming down and cascading through me as I lay on the ground of this new place. As the rhythmic music continued, I became aware that the ground on which I felt myself lying was separate from my previous world. That other world had included visual mystical imagery, Shamanic and Christian mystical experiences, and all my visions. I was now at the lowest level of a different realm, the next level up.

The following evening, as I lay in bed trying to sleep, I heard a steady breathing sound that seemed to come from inside my left ear. I turned abruptly to look at Marty, but this sound was not coming from him. With fear I got up and moved to the living room, turned on the light, and tried to divert myself by reading. This diversion did not work; the sound of breathing continued in my ear for some thirty minutes more and then suddenly stopped. For the next several days, periodically I heard rhythmic sounds of music at different times during the days and evenings. And then it ended.

This experience, which included the clear, expansive light, the music, and the breathing, was initially unclear to me. But soon, as had happened so often before, I came to understand its meaning through teachers who entered my life in the form of books.

The Clear, Expansive Light

Sogyal Rinpoche, a Tibetan Buddhist spiritual master, describes what I have come to believe was the clear light of my experience. In the *Tibetan Book of Living and Dying*, he states:

> *What is revealed as the primordial ground of our absolute nature, is like a pure and cloudless sky. This is called the dawning of the Ground Luminosity, or "Clear Light," where consciousness itself dissolves into the all encompassing space of truth. (page 47)*

Rinpoche suggests that what saints and mystics throughout history have experienced is really the essential nature of the mind . . . the Ground Luminosity. Christians and Jews call it "God"; Hindus call it the "Self," "Shiva," "Brahman," and "Vishnu"; Sufi mystics name it the "Hidden Essence"; Buddhists call it "Buddha nature." At the heart of all religions is the certainty that there is a fundamental truth, and that this life provides a sacred opportunity to evolve and to realize that truth.

He then asks why this state is called luminosity, or clear light. It has been described as "a state of minimum distraction" because all the elements, senses, and sense objects are dissolved. The dawning of the Ground Luminosity at the moment of death is the great opportunity for liberation. But only when it is established, stabilized, and integrated into our life does the moment of death offer a real opportunity for liberation. Rinpoche also cautions his students not to make the mistake of imagining that the nature of mind is exclusive to our mind only. It is in fact the nature of everything. It can never be said too often that to realize the nature of mind is to realize the nature of all things.

As I read Rinpoche's words, I could not help wondering how his description reflected the Christian mystical stage of Union—which at the time, I thought I was starting to enter. Perhaps it is analogous to the idea that as one merges with God, one becomes nothing—the body and the ego become a mere illusion. This view also seems to fit with what has been described in both Eastern and Western mysticism as Brahman and the Godhead respectively: a pure nothing, beyond the personal God, the end of all longing and desire.

Rudolf Otto (1869-1937), a German theologian and philosopher, also made comparisons between the Eastern and Western mystical traditions. In his book *Mysticism East and West,* he discussed how strong primal impulses work in the human soul, impulses that are completely unaffected by differences in geography, culture, or race. These impulses show in their similarity an inner relationship of types of human experience and spiritual life, a similarity that he believed was truly astonishing.

Divine Music

My experience with the clear light led into transcendental music. Rinpoche also discusses the clear light leading to sound:

> *From the Ground Luminosity there arises a display of sound, light and color. What is actually taking place here is a process of unfoldment, in which mind and its fundamental nature are gradually becoming more and more manifest. (page 275)*

He further states:

> *When the body or grosser levels of mind die, they are natu-*

> *rally freed and the sound, color and light of our true nature blaze out. (page 285)*

How does this apply to my life? I mused. I am aware that things are starting to shift for me. My work is feeling important to me in a new way. Does this attitude relate to what Rinpoche means by the process of unfoldment, in which mind and its fundamental nature are gradually becoming more and more manifest? Is this what the spiritual path is about—to bring into the world what one has learned, what one has become?

Indian spiritual master Muktananda in *Play of Consciousness* describes his own personal stage of meditation, which he called *nadaloka*. He describes this "nada" as divine music or sound which is heard in higher states of meditation. Upon hearing the nada, the yogi usually thinks it arises in the left ear or right ear, but actually it does not arise from the ear at all. Rather, it arises from the upper spaces of the *sahasrara*, which means the topmost spiritual center in the crown of the head. This divine music then leads to the sound of "Aum," which is called the creative voice of God.

Related to this are the words of Yogananda in *Autobiography of a Yogi*. Yogananda discusses how the creative voice of God, which he heard resounding as "Aum," is the vibration of the cosmic motor. He states:

> *These Biblical words refer to the threefold nature of God as Father, Son, Holy Ghost (Sat, Tat, Aum) in the Hindu scriptures. God the Father is the Absolute, unmanifested, existing beyond vibratory creation; . . . this Christ consciousness is the "only begotten" or sole reflection of the Uncreated Infinite. The outward manifestation of the omnipresent Christ consciousness . . . is "Aum," the word or Holy Ghost;*

> *invisible divine power, the sole causative and activating force that is heard in meditation and reveals to the devotee the ultimate truth, bringing "all things to . . . remembrance."*

Yogananda personifies the individual who moves beyond his own Hindu spiritual tradition and discovers how the Christian mystical tradition provides us with the same truths. What he really says is how Brahman, the Godhead, the Void, or Ground Luminosity are all the same and represent the vast nothingness that is beyond everything, including "vibratory creation." He then refers to Christ consciousness as manifesting itself through "Aum," the divine sound, that reveals the ultimate truth. This is how I now interpret the music I heard: another sign that acknowledges our true Christ nature.

The Sound of Breathing

As I discuss the next part of my experience—the sound of breathing—I will offer only one interpretation of it. I will quote Ken Carey, author of *The Starseed Transmissions*, which has been described by Jean Houston as "perhaps the finest example of intuitive knowledge I have ever encountered." Carey discusses the information that he received during a period of eleven days from December 27, 1978, to January 6, 1979. The words of Carey affirm much of what my journey has led me to:

> *Since the first breath of God at the beginning of all the worlds, it was preordained that Creation would exist within a rhythm of expansion and contraction. Eventually there would come a time when the physical universe would stop*

> *expanding and begin to contract. The Hindus referred to this process as the in-breathing and out-breathing of Brahma—the process through which God breathes out all of creation and then breathes it all back in again. . . .*
>
> *At this point in linear time we are very close to the middle of the present cycle, soon to reach the exact midpoint between the out-breath and the in-breath of God . . . This midpoint is called the second coming of Christ. (page 14)*

What this second coming of Christ means is further described by Carey in terms of unitive experience as follows:

> *Outside of time and space, you are one with the Creator, the All that Is, the Source. But when your consciousness moves within the context of a manifest universe, you become the Son [the Daughter], the Christ. In essence, you are the relationship between Spirit and Matter, the mediator, the bridge, the means through which the Creator relates to Creation. You are Life as it relates to planet Earth, eternity as it relates to time, the infinite as it relates to the finite. Though you presently experience yourself as a separate and fragmented species, you are in fact a single unified being, sharing the consciousness of the Creator. (page 15)*

Carey received this information in 1978. It is time for Carey's prediction to come true. In 33 A.D., a man named Jesus tried to demonstrate to the world who we really are. Unfortunately, we were not able to hear it then. Now we are being given another chance. The second coming is about all of us realizing our own Christ nature.

Throughout the world, each spiritual tradition has evolved from its own mystical roots. These mystical roots, overall, are the same. We must not misinterpret cultural differences as anything more than superficial. From these traditions we learn of a larger Reality and of our true nature. Whether we call this Reality the Great Spirit, God, the Godhead, Christ Consciousness, Buddha Nature, Allah, or Brahman does not matter. What does matter is that we identify with it. This is the only way we can believe in ourselves and our fellow humans, the only way we will be able to understand our divine nature, and the only way our troubled world will survive.

Meister Eckhart spoke the following words over 600 years ago: "Though we are God's sons and daughters, we do not realize it yet."

The time has come to realize it. Let us not put this off any longer.

PART IV

Transformation: Overcoming Polarities

Our true nature is to progress to wholeness and transformation through accessing the direct connection to an expanded reality.

CHAPTER 10
The Divine Feminine

The fruits of traveling a spiritual path are twofold: to enable seekers to reach their human potential and then to express this potential in a creative manner.

From my own developmental process as well as from my work with others who travel this path, I have learned that mystical experiences—while illuminating—do not fully prepare individuals to effectively express their newly evolving consciousness in the world. One must also engage in psychological work to eliminate ego needs and unresolved emotional issues.

Through the experiences described in this book, I entered a reality that is not accepted by mainstream society. The purpose for these experiences went beyond my own personal learning. It became clear that I was to share this reality with others. To do so, I would have to be further prepared emotionally, psychologically, and spiritually to express this material so that others would listen. And when they would not listen, I would have to learn to accept that also.

COSMIC MOTHER

To bring what I learned into my work as a psychologist has been a very challenging aspect of my journey. Worldly, psychological, and professional conflicts pertaining to mental health and mental illness, organized religion, and the meaning of good and evil became apparent as I traveled my path. Equally challenging was the confusion I felt in terms of the role I played with my clients. How was I to be when clients put me in the position of "good mother" or "bad mother"? Additional feelings related to my identity as a woman erupted from my deepest self with startling force. What was the *gender* of the spiritual figures with whom I identified? Certainly Jesus was a male. Could the Divine also be feminine? How did my self-concept as a woman influence my spiritual process? These aspects of my self had to be investigated and resolved.

The Story of Katherine

My relationship with the Divine Feminine initially came about through Katherine, a forty-two-year-old woman who has been an employee of a large electric company since graduating from high school. She is currently a supervisor. To me, Katherine's round, smiling face, beautiful blue eyes, pug nose, and interesting arrangement of freckles reflect her Irish Catholic origins. Her personality is similar to her appearance: kind and sincere.

I first met Katherine approximately three years ago. She came to me seeking psychotherapy because of problems that she was experiencing on the job. After our first session, I was startled by what she told me. She discussed how she was an only child and how her mother and father had died within two months of each other when she was only seven years old. Each of them became ill suddenly, so their deaths were shocking and unexpected.

Katherine then went to live with her aunt and uncle, a loving couple who raised her in a caring way. She became very close with them and attended parochial school and church regularly, but recalls that she was never able to cry for her parents. If she did, her aunt would also start to cry, and Katherine quickly learned that she should not express those deep, sad feelings. Her new family believed that Katherine should be strong and look forward, not backward—and so she did.

Our therapeutic relationship moved slowly. I soon discovered that it was difficult for her to express emotions. In spite of the problem that Katherine had in expressing her emotions, I was impressed with the efforts she was making in her therapy, and I was also aware that she was gradually beginning to trust me. As our relationship deepened, Katherine began to be fearful. I first started to notice this during the times I was preparing to leave on vacations. Katherine confided that she was afraid I would die. One can readily see how Katherine transferred her early trauma with her parents onto me.

As Katherine's process continued, she experienced the emotions connected to the loss of her parents—particularly her mother. As this occurred, her relationship with me became more intense. I understood this and helped her work through her feelings of fear that I would die.

While all these relationship issues were coming to the surface, Katherine began to do breathwork and had dreams and visions that focused on Mary. She referred to Mary as the Blessed Mother. Katherine was letting herself feel the pain and grief associated with her mother's premature death. As she slowly began to trust that I would be there for her, she could also trust that the Divine Mother would be in her life. This enabled her to start to move in the direction of her spiritual nature.

At about this time, Katherine announced that a friend of hers invited her on a trip to Fatima, Portugal. This is where Mary had made an appearance to three young village children in 1917. It has since become a place visited by people throughout the world. Katherine was very excited about what she called her upcoming spiritual pilgrimage.

Upon returning from Fatima, Katherine discussed with me her wondrous experience there with the Divine Mother. As she sat in the chapel at Fatima, she had a strong feeling that Mary was with her. And then as she recited the Rosary with tears streaming down her cheeks, she reported how the Divine Mother gave her a message to protect me. She described that Mary also said that Katherine would be used as an intermediary to make contact with me.

What a complex challenge this was turning out to be! How should I deal with the idea that Katherine believed that she was going to be the intermediary for Mary to make contact with me? What of my role as professional psychologist? This was taking me to a place I had never been before.

From my own mystical experiences I had learned that we can obtain information from images of spiritual figures. But how could I relate to *Mary*? Somehow a relationship to Jesus made more sense to me. My personal experience with my own mother had been complex and difficult, largely because of my parents' divorce. I had never had a strong female figure in my life whom I could learn from or depend on. Rather, it had been males who had been my mentors. I had no relationship to Mary. Catholicism felt alien to me.

But there was Katherine—so clear and strong in her conviction that Mary was working through her in order to make contact with me. I accepted Katherine's experience and the truth it represented for her. However, at a personal level, it remained difficult for me to accept.

A Shift in Consciousness

During this period, I came upon several references to Divine Mother energy. *Hidden Journey* by Andrew Harvey was particularly helpful to me. Harvey, a writer and philosopher from India, was educated and lived in England. This book describes his relationship with his guru, a young woman also from India known as Mother Mira.

The idea of having a "guru" is one that is troublesome for many Westerners. It is the antithesis of what good mental health is about in our society. The concept of people being independent and making their own decisions seems to be antithetical to having slavish devotion to another called guru. I believe this confusion exists because most people do not really understand what guru means. Guru means *through darkness to light*, and, simply, a guru is a person who is a very highly evolved individual on his or her spiritual path. A guru is a true spiritual teacher who by the example of his or her own purity and Divine being, can guide students to truth and the realization of God.

In *Hidden Journey*, Harvey speaks with his guru, Mother Mira:

> *I know who you are, Ma. You are the Force that can unify the world. You are the force that is creating the new evolu-*

tion. *You have come to us as a tender, simple Indian girl, so no one can be afraid of you. You speak in the universal language of love and silence, so what you say can pierce all dogmas, all cultural differences, all laws.*

"I am here," Ma said. "Those who want to see can see. Everything that can be done to open the mind of the world is being done."

. . . Harvey asked Ma, "If I had gone to Rome and was Christian, then you would have taught me through Christ?"

"Yes."

He then understood: "You have come to give the Light to all people, so all can awaken in whatever way they choose, in whatever situation or society or religious discipline they find themselves." (pages 184 and 194)

In *Daughters of the Goddess*, Linda Johnsen also describes how Indian scriptures and sages call ultimate reality "she." Johnsen states:

The sages are not all implying that divinity is female. This would be as absurd as the Western notion that God is male. Formless consciousness is as genderless as it is bodiless and thoughtless. Nevertheless, from ages immemorial, sages have observed that that which substands the universe behaves like a mother. It manifests the worlds out of its own womblike essence. It fosters life. The forms it projects are beautiful, and when we err against its laws, it patiently cor-

> *rects us. The sages look at this apparent actor of actionless being and call it that most beautiful and most primal of Sanskrit words: "ma." (page 188)*

I became more comfortable accepting the role of Mary in my life when I understood that she is the manifestation of Divine Mother energy and as a result, teaches her children through any of the religions, any of the gods, any holy teacher.

COMMUNICATION WITH THE DIVINE FEMININE

The most frequent, continual ways that Mary has contacted me has been through my mind, consciousness, and physical manifestations. Sometimes such communications would occur when my thoughts and activities were elsewhere, and messages coming from the deepest parts of myself would spontaneously burst forth into my consciousness. At other times, I would ask her silent questions during moments of quiet meditation. Her answers fill many of my notebooks.

Much of Mary's communication with people over the last century has been to give warnings pertaining to the state of the world and the actions that must be taken to improve things. While her messages to me have included universal knowledge and ways to help heal our planet, primarily she has assisted me in developing myself spiritually, personally, and in my work with others. In spite of my initial resistance, contact with Mary through (1) intercessors, (2) signs and miracles, and (3) travel, has become very real for me. Slowly but surely I allowed myself to trust the Divine Mother energy that had been coming to me in these varied ways. One might understandably wonder how I became aware that this information was coming from Her; I will tell my story and the reader can come to his or her own conclusion.

Through Intercession

Webster's dictionary defines intercession as "an interceding meditation or prayer on behalf of another." Catholicism places much emphasis on this concept, from the priest who hears confession and absolves the sinner from guilt, to the pope who acts as the earthly connection between Christ and humanity. It is also a universal practice in the Catholic church for the parishioners to invoke the prayers of the saints who are no longer living. The Council of Trent indicated that the saints in heaven pray for people and stated that their prayers are of intercession. St. Paul said that Jesus wishes that we should have recourse to Mary for intercession, and Pope Leo XIII in 1883 proclaimed that all graces come through Mary; she is the mediatrix of all graces.

The role of intercession clearly is a major theme in the tenets of Catholicism. And since Mary is considered to be the mother of all people, her powers of intercession for those who turn to her are believed to be very strong. I find it interesting that my contact with Divine Mother energy, as it came through Mary, was first initiated through Katherine as intercessor. In spite of the fact that I struggled with this concept, I soon realized that my relationship with Mary could not be easily dismissed.

Katherine as Intercessor

My spiritual experiences encountered during the three years that I practiced breathwork never left me. It became very clear that I would incorporate this powerful practice into my work with others as I assisted them in traveling a psychospiritual path. As a result, I lead small breath workshops for my clients monthly, and then meet with them individually in order to help them understand and integrate their breathwork experiences.

One particular breath workshop I conducted is relevant to this part of my spiritual journey. In a moment, it catapulted me out of my role as a therapist and caused me instead to abruptly and shockingly connect with the deepest part of my soul. The workshop was held at a rustic retreat center in the Pocono Mountains of Pennsylvania. It was a five-day retreat that enabled participants to live away from home and not be distracted by work, family, or other day-to-day activities. Twelve participants and I gathered during a hot spell in the month of June.

During the first breathwork session, the participants lay on their mats with their eyes closed. As I walked among each of the breathers and their respective sitters, I observed that they were experiencing a variety of emotional states. Some seemed at peace, others were more emotional, and their activity level as expressed through physical movement also gave clues to their experiences. During the beginning phase of the breathing experience, I did not intrude on the participants' processes. Only if clients seemed to be experiencing difficulty did I attempt to assist them to release the energy that was keeping them blocked. I did this through light body work, and at times their sitters assisted in the process.

During Katherine's breathing session she smiled, looked angelic, and glowed. Even with her eyes closed, her face held a beatific look that drew me to her. Several of the other sitters noticed her also, and at one point several of the people who were not doing the breathing were standing around her, mesmerized by what appeared to be a sacred experience for her.

Two and a half hours later the lilting music began to wind

down. I knelt down to chat briefly with each person as he or she gradually came back to a more worldly state of consciousness. Some were feeling very positive and shared with me their images, excitement, and insights. Others were more subdued, and with tears filling their half-opened eyes, they expressed what they were feeling and what they learned. When I knelt down to Katherine, she opened her eyes. They were wide, appeared bright blue, and were sparkling. She smiled at me directly. "The Blessed Mother welcomed me to heaven," she said. "There, my parents, the Blessed Mother, and I looked down to see you, Judith, here on earth. Mary made me an angel and told me to protect you and be here for you whenever you needed me."

I smiled back at Katherine and thought to myself that she was telling herself what she wanted to believe. At the same time, I was struck by the intensity of this experience for her.

The Challenge of Dennis

During this extended workshop, participants had the opportunity to have four breathing sessions. At the next session, on the following day, Dennis, a client I had been working with for about four months, was unsettled. Before he began his breathing, he told me that he was feeling a great deal of rage and anger rising within him. Dennis is a handsome, thirty-four-year-old successful businessman. He is highly intelligent and has classic chiseled features and dark, wavy hair. Unfortunately, he experienced a traumatic childhood comprised of emotional abuse from relatives. His relationship with his parents was difficult—particularly with his mother. During my previous individual therapy sessions with him, I had discovered a strong ambivalence on his part regarding his feelings toward me. Some of the time he was positive and trusting. At these times he expressed emotions, conveyed a strong belief in a spiritual reality, and gained understanding through his intense mystical experiences. He was strongly committed to the process, and to our relationship and work together. There were other times when Dennis was quite different. He would lack trust in me and in his spiritual process, and seemed totally disconnected from his emotions. Rational thought, science, and the intellect became his gods. I recognized these different parts of his personality and believed that his "approach-avoidance" behavior towards me represented, at least in part, unresolved conflicts with his mother.

Now, as Dennis lay down on the mat at the beginning of the second breathing session, he closed his eyes and almost immediately his body contorted. It was clear that he was experiencing much anxiety. I then conducted a short relaxation exercise for the people who would be doing the breathing work.

As the music began, people moved into deeper states of consciousness. It appeared that Dennis also moved into a state of deep consciousness; his earlier experience of restlessness and agitation led him into a state where he seemed ready to erupt. As I knelt over to help comfort him, his voice exploded and he shouted, "Boy, does it hate you, Judy!" With that, I felt an invisible energy shoot from his body and knock me over.

At that moment, I could not think clearly. The power of that unknown force that blasted through me caused me to feel as if my vital life energy was gradually draining away.

Katherine, who was a sitter during this particular session, immediately threw herself on top of me. As her body enveloped mine, she frantically whispered that she would protect me—as the Blessed Mother had instructed. Weak and helpless, I could do nothing but absorb her warm energy. Meanwhile, my assistant, Larry, and several sitters rushed over to hold Dennis down. They assisted him to walk out of the room to a safe place. Dennis at this point was not clear about what had occurred, and when he returned to his usual state of consciousness, he expressed concern for my welfare.

The workshop stopped at this point. Larry made sure that several people stayed with Dennis until he felt better and then came back to help Katherine and me. Everyone else in the workshop was told to take a break for the next hour.

Katherine was praying frantically to Mary to spare my life. In spite of my physical weakness, I recognized that she was once again being confronted with her greatest fear: I might die as her parents had. Immediately, I sat up and told her that I would be all right and she need not worry. As I began to support Katherine, I felt my strength returning, and within an hour the group was reconvened.

I spent the balance of the afternoon encouraging all participants to express their feelings about what transpired, and I attempted to make everyone feel more comfortable. In spite of my efforts, the effect it had on me, on Dennis, on Katherine, and on the other participants was very strong. I couldn't help but wonder why this traumatic event occurred on June 18, which was my birthday. It took many months for me to begin to gain clarification.

The period after the workshop remained difficult for me. I continued to ask myself how an energy force that I couldn't see or understand could have a power that was strong enough to throw me down and deplete me of my life energy. I had never experienced anything like that before. What did it mean and who could I talk to? The only other people who would believe such a thing was possible were my clients—because they witnessed it. But I felt that my obligation was to be present, focused, and helpful to them in dealing with their anxiety and confusion about the incident. On a personal level, I spent quite a bit of time trying to make sense of it all. What was the nature of this energy and why did it seem to come after me? What is the role of darkness and light as it presents itself in my work?

After the workshop, Dennis and I met several times for individual sessions. In spite of still being unsettled about the incident, I tried to support him. I remember the moment when I asked him more about the incident. He was sitting on my sofa, calm and relaxed. His eyes gazed out the large glass window overlooking the green foliage that enveloped the woods on a sunny afternoon. "Dennis, what do you think that strong energy was?" I asked. He continued to look at the trees without answering. I recalled the words that he spat at me moments before the attack. I asked him again—more directly this time. "What were you referring to, Dennis, when you exclaimed, 'Boy, does it hate you, Judy' "? His piercing, dark eyes stared deeply into mine, and with no expression or affect he stated: "It was Hitler energy."

In that moment time stopped for me. When I pulled myself together, I learned from Dennis that he was preparing to visit a close friend now living in Germany who previously had been involved in a neo-Nazi group in this country that supported Hitler's views.

After several weeks of intense personal and professional conflict, I decided to terminate my work with Dennis. He accepted my decision. In the months that followed, I learned that Dennis was a very important teacher for me.

Intercession through Stephen

In addition to Katherine, another intercessor came into my life. My relationship with Stephen extends over a twelve-year period. Stephen is a skilled construction engineer who heads a contracting business. His work ranges from building homes to resolving small household problems. Shortly after moving into our home, Marty and I contacted him to help us with a maintenance problem. Over the years our relationship evolved into a friendship. Stephen, like Katherine, is Roman Catholic and, with his wife and three children, is active in their church and in the city's Catholic community. At his yearly Christmas parties, I have met numerous priests who are his friends.

Looking back at our relationship, I am struck by the many times that he has come to my rescue at just the right time. I remember one cold winter day when I returned home to discover Marjie's parakeet lying dead at the bottom of its cage. Marjie had left the bird with me for safekeeping when she went away to college. I was upset, first, because it died, and second, because I would be unable to dig a grave in such hard, icy ground. As I stood perplexed, Stephen suddenly drove up to check on some work that he had completed earlier. When he learned of my dilemma, he took a shovel from his red truck and dug a grave so that I could bury Marjie's bird.

Then there was the time that Marty and I brought back a *spirit house* from a trip to Thailand. Spirit houses are intricately carved (about the size of birdhouses), and are placed outside homes by Thai people in order to divert evil spirits. We saw it as an interesting work of art, and upon arriving home we wondered where we were going to display it. As we remained confused about what to do with this small wooden structure, Stephen arrived to drop something off—and when we showed him the spirit house, he disclosed that he had just seen a television program that reviewed in detail the meaning and history of spirit houses. He learned the direction they should be facing in relation to the sun, how they should be placed, and other details. Needless to say, Stephen proceeded to build the perfect stand for this structure and placed it in just the right spot on our lawn.

Another example of Stephen's "good works" occurred one day when I was out of the house and he was doing some work in the garage. He noticed water starting to seep under the door that connected the laundry room to the garage. As he made his way into the laundry room, he discovered water shooting out from the water heater with great force. Our dachshund, Eggroll, was in the laundry room at the time with both doors closed. Stephen knew where to turn off the water and prevented a major flood from drowning Eggroll and washing away the lower level of our house (which includes bedrooms and a family room).

I could give many other examples of Stephen's timely presence and of his preventing everyday catastrophes from happening, but these few should suffice for now. The role that he played in my life during the last year has been profound in another way. He has been the intercessor that has brought Mary to me in a manner that I could no longer turn from.

COMMUNICATING THROUGH SIGNS AND MIRACLES

Manifestations

Stephen and I have periodic, informal conversations on a wide variety of subjects. He is a man of diverse talents and interests. He combines excellence in engineering and technology with knowledge in such topics as history, culture, philosophy, and spiritual traditions.

One afternoon he patched part of our roof after a tree limb crashed onto it. Afterwards, we relaxed over a cup of coffee at the kitchen table. As I sat with Stephen that afternoon, I found myself tentatively mentioning that I had been having spiritual experiences that seemed to be Catholic in nature and that I was somewhat confused as to why they were happening. I did not get any more specific than that, and Stephen did not ask any more questions. He smiled, however, and said that the roots of Catholicism were based in Judaism and that Jesus and Mary were Jewish themselves. Of course, I thought. Why had I forgotten to make that connection?

About a week later, during the day while I was working with a client, Stephen rang my doorbell. He apologized for interrupting me, appeared shaky and pale, and said that something unsettling had just happened. He reported that while doing construction work in a church that morning he found a large metal cross buried in a wall. He showed it to the priest of that church and was told that it probably was worn by a priest some forty to fifty years ago. This particular cross was typically used to bring light and protection to the priest and to people with whom he closely worked. Stephen then mentioned me to the priest, saying that he had a Jewish friend who was a psychologist who had been having spiritual experiences of a Catholic nature and who, further, was feeling somewhat uneasy about it all. They both agreed that since Stephen found the cross, it was his to do with as he wanted. Stephen decided to give it to me in order to bring me protection as I worked spiritually with others, and the priest agreed that this would be all right.

Stephen left the church, put the cross in his truck on the front passenger seat, and then drove to a restaurant. He locked his truck and went in to have lunch. His intention was to then stop by my house and give me the cross. When he returned to his truck after lunch, the doors remained locked, and when he unlocked them and slid into the driver's seat, he noticed that the cross was not there, but in its place was an unusual looking rosary made of blue-gray yarn with a tarnished golden cross hanging from it and a very small leather—bound book of Catholic prayers entitled *Garden of the Soul*.

Stephen was so shocked that he drove back to the church to

explain to the priest what occurred. The priest identified the rosary as having been made by priests and nuns who were held prisoners in the German concentration camps during World War II. The blue-gray fabric was made from the yarn of their striped uniforms, and such a rosary was now considered an important religious object. It was made in the camps and was grasped tightly by Catholic priests and nuns during their last moments in the gas chambers.

As Stephen presented these objects to me, he said with conviction that he and the priest knew they were for me. The rosary, in particular, made during the Holocaust, was a way of bringing my Jewish identity to the spiritual experiences I was having with Jesus and Mary. The priest did not understand why the cross had disappeared or why the rosary and the prayer book had manifested—but he believed it was a miracle.

After Stephen left, I held the rosary and prayer book. It was one thing to have visions, but the physical manifestations of such objects left me unable to form any coherent thoughts or emotions. Could there be a relationship between this rosary, made in a concentration camp, and the Hitler energy that attacked me through Dennis in the workshop?

Why was I feeling so overwhelmed? My spiritual journey had provided me with direct experience and knowledge pertaining to the unity of all things. I had learned early on about the relationships between mind and matter. Synchronicities represent aspects of the material world entering into play with the deepest regions of the psyche or consciousness. I recalled how consciousness merges with matter during periods of intense transformational change; the energy within is so strong that it erupts into the external world with the force that is necessary to create and affect matter. I also thought about the spiritual implications of all this. As discussed earlier (see Chapter 6), synchronicities imply that the script is written and that it operates in relation to a divine intelligence. Mysticism and physics are related. The mystic sees the unity of all things and the ways that one can transcend the individual self and find enlightenment.

There were several things about this experience, however, that made it very difficult to accept. First, the physical manifestation of religious articles felt miraculous to me. At the same time, they brought up deeply imbedded feelings of unworthiness within me. How could an ordinary person like me be having such extraordinary experiences? Second, unresolved conflicts concerning organized religion came up again for me. I was born Jewish—how could I be receiving holy objects that were Catholic in origin? Finally, how would psychiatry and the mental health system interpret such an experience? The terms "religious ideation," "magical thinking," "ideas of reference," "psychoses," "craziness," "coincidence," and even "dishonesty" came to me. Persons with serious mental illness are forced to live in a reality that is defined by psychiatry. Reality in these terms means that everything must be proven, related to cause and effect, and targeted toward such areas as independent living, social skills, vocational rehabilitation, and pharmaceutical elimination of delusions and hallucinations.

I could imagine the glaze that would come over a psychiatrist's eyes if I were to describe these miracles. If I showed the objects, I would probably be suspected of stealing them. Deep sadness enveloped me when I thought of the vast numbers of mentally ill patients who were isolated with their experiences. I could not discuss this with any of my professional colleagues.

Father John

I called Stephen and asked him if he thought the priest who identified the rosary would meet with me. Stephen arranged the meeting and then called to tell me another miracle had occurred. He opened up his locked truck in the morning to find a large silver medal of Mary on his front seat. This time he knew it was for him. He believed that Mary gave him this medal because he carried out his role as her messenger.

As I knocked on the door of the rectory the next day, I was greatly relieved to find a smiling Stephen opening the door and ushering me inside. "I'm so nervous," I exclaimed.
"I figured as much," he said. "That's why I thought I'd come."

As I looked around, I observed lovely rose-colored silk sofas and chairs alongside handsome mahogany furniture. The living room and dining room separated by a small center hall, radiated warmth and graciousness. Father John, a slight man with balding gray hair and sparkling blue eyes, suddenly appeared. With a genuine smile and outstretched hand he invited me into his study, and we each sat in a black leather chair on either side of his large, solid wooden desk. Stephen waved good-bye and with a wink closed the study door and left the house.

My meeting with Father John lasted several hours. During that time, I cried, experienced affirmation, and felt wonderment. It was hard to believe that I was sitting here with this priest, sharing such deeply moving experiences, but yet I needed to do it. I was seeking some kind of assurance.

The major points that Father John made were that the disappearance of the cross and the reappearance of the fabric rosary and tiny prayer book were indeed miracles. He believed that Stephen was the intercessor in this case and was rewarded with the medal of Mary. He also believed that the Hitler energy that threw me over was real. Father John saw the holy objects as a protection. He was unsure what their exact meaning was, but had no doubt they were for me alone—and that their meaning would become clear at a later time.

He told me to live a normal life with my family and friends, but also to spend time with people who could understand and support my profound spiritual experiences. He felt I was indeed guided by Spirit and needed to continue working with people as I had been doing. He said as Stephen was an intercessor for me, so was I playing this role with my clients—helping them open to the Divine. Father John pointed out the need for me to be prudent and to learn to be very clear when working with people at such strong energy levels. When interpersonal difficulties exist between me and someone with whom I'm working, their reactions during altered states of consciousness could be intensified and problematic. While Father John accepted my opinion that Dennis was a good person, he stressed that it was important that I learn to discern between the person and the energy. And when I am able to acknowledge the existence of such energy, I must learn to protect myself from it.

My meeting with the priest helped me to integrate all that had occurred. During the next months while engaged in an inner exploration to further provide me with insight, Father John's support encouraged me on my way.

Communicating through Travel

I made two trips during this period where contact with Mary occurred. This contact was neither expected nor planned-but it happened nonetheless.

Our Lady of Guadeloupe

The first trip involved my giving several lectures at a conference for mental health professionals. This conference was targeted to those clinicians who work with schizophrenic and other serious mentally ill individuals. My talk focused on the spiritual and mystical experiences of those who are diagnosed as psychotic. It took place in Albuquerque, New Mexico. During my free time, as I toured the town, I found myself by chance walking by a small chapel dedicated to Our Lady of Guadeloupe. There in the small enclosed outdoor chapel was a statue of a dark Madonna. I was the only person there at the time, and I let myself feel her divine presence in the heat of that sultry afternoon.

Historically, Mary appeared to Juan Diego at Guadeloupe, near Mexico City, in 1531. By appearing here to an Indian, speaking to him in his own language, and calling for a place of worship on Indian soil, Mary is believed by these native people to be their spiritual mother.

Through further research, I discovered that throughout Europe—especially Eastern Europe, but also in Spain, Switzerland, France, and Italy—there are other black Madonnas. And during ancient times, black Goddesses ruled Egypt and Africa, and from there, much of the rest of the world.

Our Lady of Guadeloupe helped me to think about Mary in ways that go beyond Catholic reference. Divine Mother energy has become truly universal for me, and represents the strength, power, and divinity of the feminine.

Ephesus

Three months after my trip to New Mexico, Marty and I decided to visit Istanbul for a short holiday. We chose this Turkish city because we heard it was exciting and was recognized as the one place in the world where East meets West. What we heard turned out to be true, and Istanbul proved to be a wonderful experience. There, modern technology blends gracefully with ancient Islam rituals and belief. Every few hours the Blue Mosque in the center of the old town sounds a call to prayer that brings this cosmopolitan city to a standstill. The call to prayer that comes through powerful electronic amplifiers sounds like an intense wailing chant coming from the depths of the soul.

Once in Turkey, we learned of the town of Ephesus, just outside of Istanbul. Ephesus is primarily known for its extraordinary archeological ruins that go back thousands of years. There is also a chapel that has been built to stand on the site of what has come to be known as "the house of the Virgin Mary." The story is that Jesus, during the last moments of his life, entrusted his mother to his disciple John. After the crucifixion, John brought Mary to Ephesus. This information came from a bedridden paralytic nun, Katerina Emmerich, living in Italy in the late 19th century. She began having visions in her bed, which she had not left for twelve years. She gave detailed information of the remains of the house of the Virgin Mary. In 1891, a research team followed her directions and was led to the area. They saw that the place called "Panaya Kapulu" by the local people was the house of the Virgin Mary as told by the nun. Further research showed the foundations of the house were from the first century. The house was restored in 1950 and brought to its present state. The building is a small, domed structure in a beautiful wooded setting. In 1961, Pope John XXIII proclaimed it a place of pilgrimage.

Once again I found myself in a small chapel in another part of the world looking at a statue of Mary. As I walked out of the chapel towards the garden, I saw a Greek Orthodox priest leading a service for about two dozen Japanese tourists who had made a pilgrimage to this holy place.

With tears filling my eyes, I once again felt the universal connection to the Divine Mother and was grateful that I was guided to this place.

Energy from higher realms can heal.

CHAPTER 11
Healing at Auschwitz: The Wall Came Down

The rosary that I received through Stephen enabled me to realize what it has meant for me to be Jewish. I have also questioned my true feelings about the Holocaust. Why have I been having spiritual experiences in recent years involving Jesus and Mary?

In Catholicism, the rosary is a form of prayer. At Fatima in 1917, Mary urged frequent recitation of the rosary for the conversion of humanity. The beads of the rosary can be made of any material, ranging from ivory or pearl beads custom—made for wealthy nobility, to plain fabric beads fashioned by the simple poor. As I contemplated the rosary beads that mysteriously came into my life, I observed that these beads were evenly spaced on the bluish-gray fabric. A tarnished gold cross dangled from it, and on the back of the cross, neatly engraved, were the words Roma and Italy.

Since receiving the rosary, I have learned that approximately three million Catholics were killed in the concentration camps during World War II because of their religious beliefs. Many were priests and nuns. And as I learned how the bluish-gray fabric beads were created from concentration camp uniforms, I felt a connection, a kinship between Jews and Christians. Jesus and Mary were Jewish; at our deepest roots we are the same. Politics, power needs, and human confusion split us apart two thousand years ago. How long must we hold on to this distorted picture of reality?

Recently, at a breath workshop that I conducted, one of the participants shyly described how he visualized himself as a disciple of Christ and wondered, "How can that be? I'm Jewish!"

"Why shouldn't that be?" I asked. "So was He."

As these thoughts and feelings have begun to settle, I understand how the theme of the Holocaust has been playing out for me during the last number of years.

My daughter Marjorie attended the University of Wisconsin and made a decision to study abroad during her junior year. This is an accepted practice at many colleges today, and when I first heard about it, I thought it sounded like a worthwhile opportunity. What I wasn't prepared for was her choice of where she wanted to visit. The year was 1988, and she decided that she wanted to go to Budapest, Hungary.

The Universities of Wisconsin and California at Berkeley had recently begun a student exchange program with a university in Budapest, then called Karl Marx University. This was before the fall of communism. When I first heard about her plan to go there, I felt somewhat hesitant. Yet before I knew it, Marjie was behind the Iron Curtain. And it turned out to be a very meaningful experience for her, and for Marty and me as well.

Marjie lived for the year with a Hungarian woman and her daughter in their apartment, and Marty and I spent our

Thanksgiving holiday visiting them. Ava, Marjie's Hungarian "Mom," researched the ingredients of a typical American Thanksgiving meal, and we were touched by the efforts she went to and the compromises she had to make, given the lack of such food in a communist country at that time. Instead of turkey, we had chicken accompanied by pickled turnips and other Hungarian delicacies. It was a wonderful time, some of it spent touring the countryside with Marjie as well. When we left, it was an emotional good-bye.

For much of the year, whenever she had an opportunity, Marjie spent her time traveling to neighboring cities. One such trip toward the end of her stay was to Cracow, Poland. Once there, she toured the Auschwitz concentration camp right outside Cracow. She later said that it was an opportunity for her to experience her roots in an intense, meaningful way. It was important to her that we should visit Auschwitz as well.

About a year later, we followed her advice and flew to Berlin to begin our journey to Auschwitz. It was November 1989, and I bought a warm black coat for the trip, thinking that it would be appropriate for me to be clothed in darkness. Our itinerary for this week-long trip was to fly to Berlin, take an overnight train to Warsaw, spend a few days touring Poland's countryside, stay another day at Auschwitz, and spend our final weekend in Berlin before flying home.

Once we had arrived in Berlin, our first activity was to visit the wall which then divided the city. As we walked alongside it, we were startled to see the sharp contrast between the colorful graffiti sayings written in many languages on the Western side of the wall, and the East German police, with weapons in hand, guarding their side of the wall, which was devoid of any inscriptions. As we peered over the wall onto the East German side, again a dissimilarity could be seen between the tall, gray, lifeless buildings on the Eastern side and the bustling, cosmopolitan, funky feeling of the West.

Walking among the Germans was an uncomfortable process. I could not help but feel a tightness in my chest each time I saw an older person, particularly someone who had a classic blond, blue-eyed Aryan look. I wondered what each of these people was doing during World War II and what their feelings were toward their Jewish neighbors who were herded away by the Nazis. Where were my compassionate feelings? I wondered. One should not blame a whole group for the evil of its leader. And yet, I remained very uncomfortable.

Riding the train through the countryside of Poland was a pleasant experience. As we observed the sloping green pastures, the women with babushkas, and the farm animals, I found myself moving into a more tranquil place. I even allowed myself to acknowledge that my grandmother was born in Poland and that I had roots in this country.

When we arrived in Warsaw, we were aware of much commotion. People were running through the streets, exclaiming how the wall separating East and West Berlin had just come down. The people of Germany were once more united. What an incredible happening—of all the times for us to have made this trip! Now we would be able to be part of this historical event—but first we were going to make our way to Auschwitz.

As we walked onto the tree-lined street with its attractive brick buildings, the only evidence of its true nature was the sign that bore its name—Auschwitz. Beside it was another sign with a slogan that, when translated, said, "Work will make you free."

A middle-aged man who spoke English met us in the office to say that he would be our guide. It turned out that during World

War II he was a Catholic Polish boy living in Cracow who was himself a survivor of Auschwitz. Mr. Tiaseki had spent most of his adult life working through his early trauma by talking to visitors from around the world. He told us later in the day that his job for the three years that he was a prisoner was to take dead bodies from the gas chambers and place them in the ovens.

We spent almost eight hours with him on this gray cold day. There were virtually no other tourists there and we were able to examine the barracks, lavatories, and other facilities in excruciating detail. There is also a museum on the grounds, and there we examined such things as photos of prisoners, drawings made by the children, personal items taken from the victims, their shaved hair, and so forth. We also saw a documentary film that included the actual liberation of the survivors and their condition at that time.

Mr. Tiaseki walked us across the field to Buchenwald, the death camp next door to Auschwitz that was built at the end of the war. Hitler's "final solution" was the total annihilation of all European Jews. This is where Mr. Tiaseki worked as a boy. We observed where people were killed by poisonous gas in the showers and then were burned in the ovens. We were shown the segregated male, female, and children's barracks at Buchenwald where the prisoners awaited their fate, the showers, and the large smoke stacks that once gave off the fumes from the ovens.

As we walked through the desolate fields on this gray day, feeling sick and hollow inside, Mr. Tiaseki pointed out one of the many pits where people's bodies were thrown after they were shot. This form of extermination operated concurrently with the ovens. The intent was to let the bodies decay and ultimately become part of the earth. He pointed out that there were still bone chips that could be found in the soil. As I stooped over and dug out some of these chips with my hands, I felt that I was on sacred ground and carefully and lovingly put them in a compartment of my purse for safekeeping.

Upon saying good-bye to Mr. Tiaseki at the end of this long day, my eyes filled with tears. We had been through a process together that I would remember for the rest of my life.

Marty and I walked wordlessly through the gates of Auschwitz to our rented car. As we drove through the Polish countryside, I became aware of an anger turning into a boiling rage within me. The bone chips that I was carrying were my ancestors. How could the German people have allowed such a thing to happen to millions of people? Suddenly, the thought of going back to Berlin felt upsetting. Who cared if the wall had come down?

We stopped to have dinner at a restaurant as we made our way to the train station. I became aware of how all the customers were fair and that there was not a Jewish—looking face in the place. Of course not, I thought. There are virtually no Jews in Eastern Europe anymore. One man continued to stare at us. Finally, he came over and in very broken English asked where our ancestors were from. I became uncomfortable and lowered my eyes. My stomach started to churn.

"Are you Jude?" he asked with a jeer. Marty and I got up, paid for our uneaten meals, and left.

We finally arrived at the train station. The Berlin wall had come down, it was Friday night, and the station was overflowing with people. As we got on the train and managed to find a seat together, it became apparent that this was not going to be a typical train ride. There would be many local stops in East German towns, and at each stop more and more people pushed on. The closer we got to Berlin, the greater the crowds. Soon there was no space for movement. As my eyes fell on the faces, I noticed several commonalties: blond hair turning gray, people holding bouquets of flowers for relatives they had not seen for thirty-some years, hands tightly grasping addresses and telephone numbers, and eyes filled with tears of joy, awe, and disbelief.

My eyes unexpectedly also filled with tears as I felt the emotions of these people and realized that Marty and I were on a spiritual journey—that we were moving from a place of ultimate darkness to one of light with these people. The fact that most of them were German no longer mattered. We were all human beings sharing a time of major change and of purification.

The train arrived in East Berlin, and together we all ran out, hugging each other with eyes sparkling, and feeling great joy. The East German soldiers were also crying as they stepped aside and allowed the crowds to step on free land, at last.

To be part of this extraordinary happening in Berlin was, for me, a metaphor of what it means to be fully alive. What could be more meaningful than to collectively experience at the same time the universal emotions of joy and hope for a better world? How grateful Marty and I were to be there.

The simple bluish-gray rosary has meant a great deal to me. It has fully established my common heritage with Jesus and Mary; it has helped me feel connected to the three million Catholics who were in the concentration camps alongside the Jews; it has represented the triumph of light over darkness as Marty and I traveled from the East to the West with thousands of Germans who, in those moments, were our brothers and sisters. A cabinet in my living room now displays a very special reminder of this experience. Set upon a tiny, navy-blue velvet cushion are several bone chips and pieces of the wall that came tumbling down on that day.

My conflict about being Jewish and having spiritual experiences of Jesus and Mary has been eliminated. My spiritual identity no longer has anything to do with organized religion. I have moved beyond secular Judaism and been led instead to its roots. At these roots is Christ. Here, no separations or differences exist between Jews and Christians. As a result, I am able to address clients' concerns around this issue in a manner that is clear. In addition, I no longer blame an entire culture for the Holocaust. Human evil, as it was manifested through Hitler, has occurred throughout the history of civilization in all races and cultural groups. I now understand that the Holocaust is not a tragedy only for the Jews. It represents the dark side which has always existed for humankind. The rosary—what it represents and how I received it—has brought about this healing.

An energy force can attach to our fears until these fears are acknowledged and released.

CHAPTER 12
Good and Evil

The miracle of the cross has enabled me to come to terms with my questions regarding good and evil: What is darkness and what is light? How can I make sense of the darkness I see in people, in the world, and in spiritual experience? Why are there people who show greed and violence some of the time and at other times are loving and deeply caring? Does evil really exist as a force, and if so, where is God?

The reader may recall that the three miracles that I attribute to Mary began when my friend Stephen intended to bring me a cross that he found in the wall of a church. He and Father John believed it would bring me light and protection in my spiritual work with people. Then the cross disappeared from the front seat of Stephen's locked truck, while in its place was discovered the bluish-gray rosary and the small leather-bound prayer book entitled *Garden of the Soul*.

The story of the cross, however, was not over. Approximately eight months later, during the Easter season, Stephen again appeared at my door. He said that the cross, the one which had originally disappeared, had reappeared in the attic of his home. As he and his wife were rummaging through their attic, he lifted a loose floor board and found the cross beneath it. This time he was not so shocked. The day after he found it, he came to my home, handed me the cross, and said it was now mine. When I attempted to protest, he would not take no for an answer.

The cross is approximately eight inches in height and has a dark wooden crucifix ensconced in a larger silver one. There is a raised figure of Christ being crucified on the wooden cross and a skull and crossbones under his feet. I subsequently learned that Catholicism has historically identified this type of cross as "the happy death cross." It has been used by priests as a spiritual tool to bring forth light and protection.

I feel strongly that the power and energy of this cross and its miraculous disappearance and reappearance not only guided me to deeper awareness regarding the nature of good and evil, but also helped me in the work I was doing with clients. When the cross had disappeared from Stephen's truck, I was uncertain regarding the nature of light and darkness. When it returned, I had come to understand this aspect of reality in a different way.

AN EXPERIENCE OF DARKNESS AND LIGHT

The following case is an example of how the issue of light and darkness became manifest for one of my clients, a man named Austin.

Austin, a Jewish man in his mid forties, is married to Sally, and they have a thirteen-year-old daughter named Joan. He is an administrator working in a federal agency, but his spiritual experiences began when he was a young man in college. For most of his adult life, he has tried to live in his community in a manner that blended with contemporary society. At the same time, he has been committed to following a spiritual path. For many of these years, Austin has experienced conflict as he tried to live a life that felt split between these two worlds.

Over the last few years, Austin's spiritual and mystical experiences have become highly intense. My work with him has been to help him to integrate these experiences into his everyday life. The spiritual information has come to Austin in different ways: through real-life manifestations and from messages that he has received from a visionary shaman at times when he has been in a trance state or altered state of consciousness during breathwork. Excerpts from Austin's journal demonstrate how his spiritual experiences parallel real life events.

January 15, at Breathwork

[Some of the imagery and feelings that arose during Austin's breathwork experiences]

> *I am in the Big Sky, a deep-blue, almost black, expanse of space. Silver crosses fill the sky and are floating down. I sit and watch for a long time. Then the scenery changes. I see the silver crosses at my work place, in my home, in the room here where we are breathing.*

> *Then I return to the view of the Big Sky. I am lying down. My chest cavity opens. The crosses enter my heart area, my body. They are inside me. I lie there, without any words,*

without any thoughts, with the silver crosses inside me.

Judith comes over to me and gently presses my head. With eyes closed, I see the Shaman holding a thick cord of rope that he somehow has magically twisted in the shape of infinity. The rope is glowing, flashing, pulsing with Light. I tell Judith what I am seeing, but I don't know what will happen. She leaves me to what will happen.

The Shaman is dressed in white. He is putting on clear plastic gloves. I understand he is a doctor, and I realize he is preparing for a major surgical procedure. On me.

Next, he performs the same surgery to my brain, replacing it with another Rope of Light.

Then he operates on my sexual area. It is afterwards, I feel resistance and frustration building inside me. I haven't been experiencing any sensations of the actual surgical work he is doing on me. I say: "I know this is not really happening. I don't feel anything you are doing to me." He says nothing. I see a severe look on his face, and I see he is holding a big bucket in his powerful hands. I don't know if the bucket is filled with icy cold or scalding hot water; I do know he is going to dump the contents on me. I cringe, in expectation and distress, as he turns the bucket over, and what comes out are the crosses, like glistening glorious snowflakes landing gently on my head and on my face.

This has a transforming effect on me. I feel soothed. I feel calmed. I find peace throughout my being. My resistance is gone. The Shaman continues with the operation, removing my old organs and bodily systems, and replacing them with the Ropes of Light. I lie quietly for a while, feeling, knowing the new infrastructure is here, inside me, to change me and guide me.

I feel a journey is over. Judith comes over and tells me to keep breathing. I feel the Shaman receding from me, leaving me alone.

February 1, at Home

[Austin's thoughts, in relation to a real-life trauma, as reported in his journal]

Friday morning there is ice everywhere, except for what is falling from above-heavy rain. Water surges into our home, flooding the family room, the TV room, the powder room, the laundry and storage rooms. Water enters the kitchen, threatening the living and dining rooms. Sally and I fear the effects of the flooding on our electricity and gas. We rush, almost madly, moving furniture, possessions, trying to save things until there is nothing to do but wait, and try to breathe in and out. It is a disaster. It feels like loss. It feels like death.

Yet at no time do I really doubt that in this darkness and awful drama, God is present. I know this is part of my journey.

February 2, at Home

[More thoughts following a phone conversation with me]

I speak with Judith on the phone. I understand the operation performed on me and the water pouring into my home are the same! Both were infiltrations, invasions, violations. My permission is not being requested. Major actions are being taken on me and at me without my consent. Judith says: "All you can do is surrender." All I can do is surrender.

The surgery and the flood come from the same Place. They are done by the same Actor. I know: the Shaman is an intermediary for this Actor. Judith asks: "Where is this Actor, this Being?" I come to the answer:

He (She/It) is out there . . . Who is he?

He (She/It) is God . . . He (She/It) is an extraterrestrial . . . He (She/It) is the Light . . .

At the End of the World.

March 12, at Breathwork

[Austin asking himself questions in an expanded state of consciousness]

I am ready to ask: What am I so afraid of? I answer: I am afraid of what is out there. I ask again: What am I so afraid of? I answer, I am afraid of being violated. As this answer hums in the great silence, I hear a chorus of voices quietly chant: "I am being violated." I ask again: What am I so afraid of? I answer, I am afraid of losing my self. Out of the stillness again comes the voices: "I am losing myself."

April 11, at Home

[Austin's reaction to another real-life trauma]

For about a week Sally has been aware of having problems adjusting to the light when she would open her eyes in the morning. On Good Friday—the day of darkness—her vision markedly deteriorated. Since then she has been undergoing extensive testing-many blood lettings and heart studies, an MRI scheduled for Monday to find out what lies behind her retina. And she has been undergoing much testing within—the great fear of what is happening and what may happen.

The muck in the house, the muck in Sally's eye: it is the same muck. The source of the muck in the house, the source of the muck in her eye: it is the same Source. Sally is being worked on. What is out there is intervening directly.

The fear that I have been feeling is not gone, but I am feeling different. Then I understand: I have been afraid that I will be living in this fear-state forever. But I will not be in this fear-state forever. Everything changes, always, in all ways. Doors will open, many more doors will appear. This is a transition period.

And I know I will give up the fear of losing my Self. I will give up my Self. I have no choice. Much has happened to me and in me. Much has manifested, much is still unclear, much is clear.

I have wondered: Why am I here, in this body, in this life, on this planet? Where do I come from? Where might I be going?

I have learned: The darkness and the light are intermingled, interactive, inseparable.

I know: everything is being taken care of. Everything is included.

The courage and commitment demonstrated by Austin as he developed psychologically and spiritually have caused me once again to feel respectful and humbled by this process. For Austin there are few separations now between the physical and spiritual worlds. He acknowledges that problems come to him for a purpose. He sees all experience as part of the divine plan. He knows that when he surrenders he will lose his ego self and then reach his human potential to merge and become united with God.

Over the last year, in particular, as my clients have moved into deeper parts of their processes, more challenging situations have presented themselves to me. At psychological levels, I have entered into close relationships with them and have been the recipient of their love as well as their rage. Working closely with people often brings up their unresolved emotional concerns and confusion, which can get transferred onto me as the therapist.

The spiritual levels also parallel the psychological levels. I have witnessed the transcendent experiences of my clients and have observed how negativity can course through them as well.

As I attempted to see more clearly the nature of darkness and light, I began to study the various perspectives of philosophers, theologians, and prophets throughout time. This topic has been addressed by the great spiritual traditions as well; Christianity, Judaism, and Islam have delved seriously into this area for two thousand five hundred years.

The next section offers a brief, selective review of various perspectives on the nature of good and evil. Further, I discuss the ways in which my thinking changed with the mysterious disappearance and reappearance of the cross.

SOME PERSPECTIVES ON THE NATURE OF GOOD AND EVIL

Contemporary Psychology

As a psychologist I have been trained to look at underlying causes for people's dysfunctional behavior—usually to be found in early familial patterns or socioeconomic deprivations. It is apparent that some of my clients accept the perspective that their dysfunctional and problematic behavior has justifiable causes. As such, they expect me, as their therapist, to acknowledge and be accepting of them, even when they behave in a manner that is abusive to me, themselves, and/or others.

Sometimes their energy feels very negative. The conflict for me comes when I turn away from what I know to be spiritually true—that there is a strong energy force in the universe that can attach to people's unresolved fears, anger, and ego needs. When this happens, people must have the strength and courage to face and release their negative feelings and behavior.

Organized Religion

Mainstream religious institutions often take the position that darkness exists as a separate force and that people should align themselves only with "goodness." Such a view makes sense from certain perspectives. It also, unfortunately, can influence people to repress the fears and negativity found within themselves and consequently to thwart their growth and development. If, on the other hand, individuals will acknowledge such feelings, they can then own their negative emotions, work toward letting them go, and finally move past them.

The Teachings of Jesus

Jesus' teaching is for each of us to recognize the personal darkness within. Only by recognizing one's dual nature, enduring the resulting tension, and undergoing the developmental process of acknowledging both the darkness and the light found within, can an individual develop their psychological and spiritual consciousness. Jesus wanted people to face the problem of their own dual nature, to be psychologically honest, and to unite the polarities within themselves. Jesus himself recognized that His way was not easy: "The road that leads to destruction is wide and spacious and many take it, but it is a narrow gate and a hard road that lead to life and only a few find it." (Matthew)

The narrow way to transformation means that each person must go inside to find the truth. This truth is found in the depths of one's soul. *Know thyself* lies at the heart of Jesus' teachings.

Scholars who have researched the teachings of Jesus emphasize his focus on death: "Whoever seeks to gain his life will lose it, but whoever loses his life will preserve it." (Matthew). The path of death to Jesus served as a metaphor for an internal process, a dying of the self as the center of its own concerns, and a dying of the world of conventional wisdom as the center of security and identity.

The spiritual path is an individual one that necessitates personal freedom. Mainstream institutions, on the other hand, look at the individual as needing to conform to the "collective ideal." The collective ideal by necessity varies according to the particular doctrines established by the authoritative body.

Emanuel Swedenborg

Swedenborg was a Swedish visionary born in 1688. Today he has many followers worldwide and is considered among the last of the great scholars who grew out of the Renaissance. In *Heaven and Hell* (1758), he wrote:

> *The reason spiritual balance is essentially a freedom is that it is between what is good and what is evil and between what is true and what is false. So the abilities to intend either the good or the evil, and to choose one rather than the other is the freedom granted to every individual and is not in any manner taken away. . . . It is given to the individual as a possession along with his life, the purpose being his reformation and salvation. For without freedom, there can be no reformation or salvation. (page 501)*

Swedenborg's thinking emphasized the necessity of individual growth, development, and personal freedom. He believed that people should not be told by outside authorities how to behave. Rather, they should be taught to look within so that they can make their own moral choices for spiritual evolution.

Carl Jung

Jung, the contemporary psychiatrist, agreed with both Jesus and Swedenborg regarding the nature of good and evil. He said how the fulfillment of our being requires a unified personality in which the conscious and unconscious minds act in unison and not in opposition to each other.

To find one's way to consciousness, Jung believes that people need to be driven to it by necessity. And this necessity comes when evil is encountered in such forms as pain, loss of meaning, and destructiveness. From the perspective of depth psychology, a power in life that opposes wholeness is needed for wholeness to occur.

Jung coined the term "shadow" as a psychological concept referring to the dark, feared, unwanted side of our personality. *Collective shadow* refers to darkness that often manifests itself upon a group or culture. It is not difficult to think of various collective shadows that took place throughout history. Nazi Germany, witch burnings, and the Spanish Inquisition are but a few. It takes considerable individual consciousness and wholeness to avoid a situation where our individual shadow qualities become intermingled with the collective shadow of our time and culture.

PSYCHO-SPIRITUAL INTEGRATION

The miracle of the cross brought to consciousness the residual conflicts I felt between two parts of my self, the modern psychologist and the spiritual teacher. As I assist clients on their psycho-spiritual paths, it becomes necessary for me to discern between darkness and light, both within myself and within them. There have been times when dark energy has been directed towards me, psychologically, spiritually, or in some combination of both. Some of these times I would tell myself that as psychologist I need to understand their anger and transference. Therefore, I would be unconditionally accepting, empathic, and non-confrontational. At other times, it would not be so easy, and I found myself increasingly terminating relationships with clients who I felt were unable to move past their acting-out behavior. I did not want any longer to be the target of their anger, unresolved ego issues, transference, and fear. I began to see situations and people in polarized ways. They were either on the right path or the wrong one. They were working either with me or against me.

I now work with people in a different way than I did before. I do not believe in psychopathology or psychiatry's diagnostic labels. I don't see people as either good or bad, as either well-adjusted or mentally ill. Rather, we are all a rich combination of both ends of the continuum. Struggles with darkness hold seeds for us to grow and expand into light; if we bask too long in the light, we might find ourselves back in the dark.

My question regarding the nature of good and evil has been largely resolved. Much of the time I work with others' darkness without resistance or fear. However, there are other times when I will not work with someone at a particular energy level. If their unresolved emotional issues reflect any of my unresolved issues, then I cannot be the one to help them.

In Dennis' case, there were two areas of difficulty that got projected onto me: first, his ambivalent feelings toward me because of his difficult relationship with his own mother; and second, his close friendship with someone who had previous identification and connection with a neo-Nazi group. Dennis' energy then attached itself to areas of confusion for me, conflicts around my Jewish identity and my professional role. If I had not had those conflicts, I believe that the energy he described as Hitler energy would not have had the power to knock me over.

Clearly, in spite of my experience at Auschwitz and the Berlin Wall, I still had residual fear, anger, and ambivalence about having been born Jewish. I also struggled with my professional identity; I had to become clear regarding the role I played with people, and if I acknowledged that my primary professional identity was as a spiritual guide, then I needed to have a clearer position on the nature of good and evil.

Together, Dennis' and my fears and human weaknesses created the pathway for the chaos that subsequently ensued. Each of us has our own particular vulnerabilities. A powerful energy force brought them to our attention. Dennis brought me the truth that I needed to understand. I will always be appreciative to him for this gift.

The dark and light aspects of people's psyches are partners in the Divine plan. And the energy force that attaches to the different parts of our psyches is the catalyst for our soul development. As human beings, this challenges us to evolve psychologically and spiritually. I now see an order, purpose, and higher meaning for each of our lives and for the problems that we have the ability to resolve, both individually and collectively.

A Limitation to New Age Thought

While increased attention is being directed in recent years to so-called New Age psychology and spirituality, there seems to be minimal interest in dealing with the individual and collective shadows that are inherent in human nature. Emphasis instead is targeted toward one's godly nature, finding the good in all, the light, and so forth. Surely, it is hard to find fault with this euphoric focus. However, such thinking does pose a serious limitation. Expanded states of consciousness incorporate energy that is representative of the most powerful forces of nature, of human evolution and soul development. This energy state will, by necessity, catapult unresolved emotional blockages to the surface of one's awareness.

When individuals, using various New Age methodologies, move into expanded states of consciousness, they must follow up by doing in-depth psycho-spiritual work. Such work will almost always facilitate an encounter with personal "demons"-the fears, rage, confusion, and prejudices that have accumulated over a person's lifetime.

Merely attending a spiritual conference and thinking about one's divinity is illustrative of a behavior, all too common in our culture, that seeks to acquire some result quickly, with little meaningful effort being put into that goal. Rather, it is critically important that a deeper effort be undertaken wherein individuals are assisted in confronting their personal darkness so that they will be able to reach their human potential. When individual shadows are not acknowledged or worked through, they erupt on this planet in the forms of violence, rage, destruction, and annihilation of the self.

Beyond time and space, we are one with the Divine.

CHAPTER 13
Garden of the Soul

The third miracle, after those of the rosary and the cross, manifested itself through the tiny, black leather-bound prayer book, identified as a manual of devotion. This is the book which, along with the bluish-gray rosary, had miraculously appeared on the seat of Stephen's truck in place of the cross that he had left there. The title of the book, *Garden of the Soul*, is engraved in gold on the jacket, and a gold cross is engraved on the leather cover. The book was published in London around 1920.

Over the course of a year, I became clear regarding what this little prayer book meant to me: I no longer look to other people as being necessary for my connection with Divine Mother energy. Rather, I see it now as coming to me and through me in a direct manner. Initially I needed intermediaries because of the personal conflicts I experienced with my own mother. I had been unable to accept that Divine Mother energy would seek me out with unconditional love. The little prayer book miraculously helped me to transform my way of thinking.

Through the power of the prayer book, *Garden of the Soul*, I have at last been able to merge with the Divine Feminine. In so doing, I am now whole. The path that I traveled to attain this was filled with wonder, synchronicities, and major loss.

DEATH AND REBIRTH

The next phase of this story was initiated during a vacation. Marty and I decided to take two weeks in May to visit Indonesia. Our plane landed in Singapore, and we made our way to several Indonesian islands: Bali, Lombok, and Sulawesi. As we toured the islands of Bali and Lombok, we were fascinated with the villages, the Hindu temple festivals, the mythology, and the natural beauty of the terrain. The major significance for me, however, was found in Sulawesi.

Funeral in Torajaland

Tucked away between the rugged peaks and fertile plateaus of the central islands of Sulawesi live an isolated tribe of people known as the Toroja, or "highland people." Flying into Torojaland on the tiny plane that seated nine people seemed very different from flying into the other islands that we had visited in Indonesia. As we stepped off the plane, the environment no longer felt as tropical as it did in the other islands; the high mountains combined with rolling green pastures, rice paddies, and cool weather made us feel that we had arrived in a different part of the world. The two days that we would spend in Torojaland turned out to be monumental in their own right; what I didn't know at the time was that these days would be prophetic of what was to follow in my life.

We met Luigia, our English-speaking guide at the hotel. He told us that the Torojan people lived in a "death culture." They combined ancient Shamanic practices with Christianity and were known for their elaborate, colorful funeral feasts for the dead that could last up to a week. A person would be considered dead only after the family had gathered the appropriate goods in preparation for the funeral feast. This preparation could take months. During the waiting period the deceased is regarded as merely "sick," and the corpse, which has been ritually cleansed and dressed, is fed and visited as if still alive.

For the Toroja, the funeral festivals ensure that the souls of the dead may pass to the afterworld in a manner appropriate to the status they enjoyed in this world. After these rites have occurred, the ancestors will bless the living, and the balance between the realms of the living and the dead will be preserved.

The Torojan homes completely reflect their attitude toward death. The roofs of their homes rise at both ends like the bow and stern of a boat. The roofs are always red and are representative of the boats that will eventually take them from the land of the living to the land of the dead. Coffins are placed in containers that sit next to their house, and, like the roofs, they too appear as red boats. These red boats take the corpse to mountainside family grave sites where it is placed, and its effigy in the form of a life-sized wooden puppet is installed on a high balcony overlooking the green valleys of the Torojan homeland.

As we toured the countryside with Luigia we were told that on the next day we would be honored guests at the first day of a funeral festival. As such, we found ourselves sitting with the family of a seventy-two-year-old deceased woman in an open porch facing a coffin. We drank palm wine and ate the rice cookies that were served. We also observed hundreds of people wearing black, making offerings of betelnut and fruits as they marched slowly past the coffin. The rites included the slaughter of dozens of pigs that were carried by ropes though the procession. Finally we observed the *tomabalu*, or "death specialist," ritually slaughter a water buffalo by a single stroke of the sword. Its blood was collected in bamboo containers, cooked with the buffalo meat, and distributed among the guests.

Although we were among the Toroja only for a short time, we interacted with them, climbed into caves among the bones of the dead, and were their honored guests at the first day of a funeral. The intensity of these few days was quite overwhelming. As we flew off the island, it felt as if we had descended into another world and were now leaving it. I knew that our experience among the Torojan people would be the high point of our trip.

Returning Home

Arriving in Singapore from Torojaland represented a one-day hiatus before our twenty-two-hour flight home. After our previous experiences, the cosmopolitan quality of Singapore seemed quite a contrast. Torojaland was becoming more and more surrealistic in my consciousness.

Flying back to Philadelphia after our last day in Singapore, I started, once again for reasons I did not understand at the time, to read *Hidden Journey*, the spiritual autobiography by Andrew Harvey. While reading Harvey's words pertaining to his communication with Divine Mother energy coming through his spiritual teacher, Mother Mira, I came upon these words:

> *I heard her voice say, 'I will always be here in the Garden of*

Your Soul. No force in hell or heaven can shake that now.'
(page 187)

Here was the answer to the conflict of what it meant to accept Divine Mother energy coursing through me. I had to move beyond the emotional issues that I felt with my own mother. I also had to stop disempowering myself by looking to others to bring me divinity (as, for example, to Katherine and Stephen as intercessors). Finally, it was time to fully accept my direct connection to God. If a spiritual force comes to me through Mary, in spite of my discomfort, that is the way I will accept it.

According to Mother Mira, Divine Mother energy merged with Andrew Harvey in the garden of his soul. Could this prayer book entitled *Garden of the Soul*, which came to me so mysteriously, mean the same thing for me as Mother Mira said it meant for Harvey? Could I also now acknowledge that Divine Mother energy and I were merged in the core part of myself?

The past year had brought several key events—my initial contact with Mary through Katherine, the very difficult experience I encountered with Hitler energy on my birthday, the holy objects received through the intercession of Stephen, and, finally, at this moment the shocking insight that union with the Divine Mother could take place directly through the garden of my soul. The words that I read were meaningful, but were they really applicable to me? Had I really merged with Divine Mother energy? I did not think so. The time had not yet come.

Floating Cradle

Shortly after returning home, I discovered that I needed to have surgery. There was a gynecological problem with which I had been struggling for three years, and it appeared that the time had now come for me to deal with it surgically. Even though this was a common operation, I felt threatened. The imagery of the slaughtered buffalo and other symbolic representations of the death culture where we had just been in Torojaland moved in and out of my consciousness.

My doctor looked at his schedule and said that he wanted to plan surgery for the week of June 18. June 18—my birthday, fell on a Sunday. He settled for a few days later: Thursday, June 22. Last year I had been assaulted through Dennis at the workshop on my birthday. Now it felt as if I would be assaulted again, this time through surgery.

With this upcoming surgical cloud hanging over me, I followed through with a commitment I had previously made to speak to a group of mental health professionals on the topic of schizophrenia and spiritual crises. The conference was with the same group that convened a year earlier in Albuquerque, where I had seen Our Lady of Guadeloupe. Now, a year later, the meeting was being held in Boston. My presentation went well, and I was able to place the upcoming surgery into the distant recesses of my mind. After the conference, I arranged to visit a friend in Provincetown, Massachusetts, for the weekend. She had a house on the ocean, and it seemed to me that this get-together would be a nice way to end my trip to Boston. Honey was a good friend. She had originally lived in Philadelphia and was a co-participant in the three-year breathwork group with Stan Grof. Honey would be an easy person with whom to share my concerns regarding the upcoming surgery.

The three days at Provincetown proved especially meaningful to me. Shortly after I arrived there, I met Barbara, Honey's new housemate. Barbara, who was an artist, invited me into her studio to see her work. The two paintings I immediately saw upon walking into her studio hit me like a tidal wave. The first painting portrayed three different views of a small, red boat shaped like a canoe that she had seen on the beach outside her window. She told me that the shape of the boat reminded her of a coffin, and she entitled the painting "Floating Cradle," to signify the process of death and rebirth. This red boat looked exactly like the roofs and coffin containers that I had seen in Toroja.

The next painting I saw was an abstract representation of what appeared to be a cow or buffalo. The front part of its body and head were painted red. To me this painting represented the slaughtered buffalo at the Torojan funeral.

Barbara had never been to Indonesia and certainly had no conscious knowledge of its culture when she painted these pictures. At the time I took these paintings as a positive sign in my life. My surgery would be successful and represent a death-rebirth process for me, as her title "Floating Cradle" suggested. I bought these two paintings from the artist and, upon arriving home, immediately hung them for good luck.

The Ultimate Gift

The surgery was successful, and three days later I went home to recuperate. The days I spent in the hospital were not particularly pleasant. I had pain and was trying to deal with feelings that understandably come up in the face of an invasive procedure such as surgery. Despite the initial discomfort, my healing was very rapid. A week after I returned from the hospital, Marty and I drove to the shore to relax.

It was Saturday, the first of July. I telephoned my mother upon arriving at our seaside house. She had been living at a nursing home for about five years due to a stroke that left her unable to walk. The nurse told me that my mother refused to come to the phone. According to the nurse, when my mother awakened that day she informed the staff that she would not eat or take her medicine because God came to her during the night to say that she would die on the following evening. When she heard that I was on the phone, she asked the nurse to give me the message explaining why she couldn't come to the phone.

When I expressed shock, the nurse said not to worry. They had called my mother's doctor that morning and he examined her and found her vital signs to be fine. "Call back tomorrow, Judy," she said. "Your mother is fine. She is just in an odd mood today."

At 6:30 P.M., when they brought her dinner in, once again, she calmly said she would not eat because it was time for her to die. They left and came in a few minutes later to see her eyes closed and a peaceful look on her face. My mother had passed on.

Later that night, after driving home, I went to see her before she was taken from the nursing home to the funeral parlor. She had a half smile on her face, and to me she looked more peaceful and serene than she had in years.

My mother and I had a complex relationship since her divorce, but had managed to become closer and more loving and accepting of each other during the last few years of her life. She no longer exists in my outer world. I no longer have to struggle with my identity as her daughter or be conflicted about her role as my mother. I miss her very much and now know that despite the difficulties we encountered, she loved me from the deepest part of her self.

Psychological conflicts regarding my role as my mother's daughter no longer act as barriers that prevent Divine Mother energy from filling me. I can now let myself fully accept my spiritual mother's energy in the garden of my soul. We are merged now at the deepest level. My mother gave me—through her death—the ultimate gift: she enabled me to accept and be at one with the Divine Mother. She paved the way for my transformation—she gave me my Self.

Sufi spiritual master Siddi Muhammad al-Jamal ar-Refaiss-Shadih in *The Guide of the Peace and Love to the Way of Allah* stated:

> *When you remember the Name of God, you live in the garden. There are many gardens where you reach God, but he wants you to live in the Garden of his Soul, not tomorrow, not after your die, but now. You can feel happiness and peace and you can touch Him in your hand. (page 18)*

My third conflict has cleared. Room has been made for Divine Mother energy. It is spiritual energy without emotional attachments and fears. I no longer react with emotion when clients attempt to transfer issues of their own mothers onto me. I encourage them to move beyond this so that they also can connect with the garden of their soul.

There is an order and purpose for each of our lives.

CHAPTER 14
A Transformation of Consciousness

This final chapter reviews and integrates important aspects of the spiritual journey described in this book and emphasizes the ways in which two early experiences became prophetic messages that foretold my life's work and mission.

TWO PROPHECIES

Epiphenomena

The first prophecy occurred some twenty years ago. How could I have known at the time that the unknown word "epiphenomena"—racing uncontrollably through the left side of my brain—represented mainstream psychiatric thought? Concurrently, it felt as if my deepest self was trying to catapult out of my body through the other side of my mind, thus demonstrating a need to break old boundaries in order to free my soul.

The years that followed reflected a split within me that the *epiphenomena* experience predicted. One part of me wanted to hold on to a world view that represented contemporary American thought and the theories and practice of mainstream psychology. At the same time, another part of me was trying to let go of those limited perspectives.

The path I've traveled has been guided by spirit. Initially, I encountered paranormal phenomena and explored near-death experiences and survival after death. Synchronicities then occurred, along with glimpses from the collective unconscious. As I began to acknowledge that human consciousness goes beyond consensus reality and the five senses, my world view expanded even further.

Spiritual energy began to push me to move beyond intellectual investigation. My professional life was no longer fulfilling. It seemed to me that there was no place in my work for the spirit that was so strongly influencing my life. I began the three-year Transpersonal program with Stan Grof in an effort to gain clarity.

A Russian Priest and The Tree of Life: The Second Prophecy

My first breathwork experience was confusing. Why was I visualizing an Eastern Orthodox priest bowing his head and praying to God, alongside a large tree which was "The Tree of Life"? The Tree of Life symbolizes Jewish mysticism and is described in the Kaballah as the central metaphor for the universe and every aspect of it.

After that initial breathwork experience, I began to see more clearly and to make a direct connection with other spiritual traditions. Kundalini energy, integral to Hinduism, soared through me and led to a Shamanic initiation. I was learning that all spiritual traditions lead to the same sacred ground.

The stigmata I received as I was beginning to write this book led me to a mystical life. Experiences of Christ Consciousness transformed my being. I came to understand how Jesus Christ symbolizes for the West what the Buddha and Mohammed represent for the East. Jesus' life provides us with knowledge of our human potential when we open to God energy. Merging with Christ Consciousness necessitated that I sever any residual identification that I still had to organized religion.

Divine Mother energy, as it came through Mary, crushed more of my ego and thrust me to an even deeper mystical realm than where I'd been before. My will became submerged under the force of pure spirit. Miracles became manifest, and once again I felt changed in ways that seemed unbelievable. The appearance of the rosary beads made from the uniforms of the Holocaust victims of World War II brought me in direct contact with my Judeo-Christian roots. The dualistic energies of these roots necessitated that I learn to recognize and work with the dark and light aspects of myself and others. The appearance of the "Happy Death Cross" protected and taught me how to do this. Finally, the tiny prayer book, *Garden of the Soul*, led me to accept that Divine Mother energy was coming through me.

My vision of the Russian priest next to the Jewish mystical "Tree of Life" foretold how perceived separations and differences between Jews and non-Jews would disappear for me and how the mystical roots of Catholicism and Judaism would come together in my soul.

After my mother's death, I traveled to Russia in an effort to connect with my maternal ancestral roots. My mother's father was an Orthodox Jew who was born and lived some of his life in Russia.

The last part of my trip was spent in St. Petersburg. On my last day there, before coming home, I visited an Eastern Orthodox church and saw the priest I had visualized in my breathwork, bowing his head in prayer as he handed out holy wafers to his congregants. I then visited the only synagogue that remains in St. Petersburg and discovered that it was Hasidic, which is the mystical branch of Judaism and is described in the Kaballah. Over the front door of this synagogue is engraved an image of "The Tree of Life."

From this experience I learned how life and death are interchangeable and how all our lives are predetermined, connected, and intertwined. All we have to do is look—and we shall see. The vision in my first breathwork paved the way for this realization.

MY LIFE'S MISSION

Psychology Meets Spirituality

Guiding others on their spiritual paths has affirmed for me that all individuals are filled with spirit in their core selves. I have given numerous examples of this throughout the book. When my clients make such a connection, whether it be through meditation, breathwork, dreamwork, energy exchange, or whatever, their lives change in remarkable ways. The evolutionary goal for individual growth is to make contact with one's core self and then to work with the unresolved psychological and emotional problems that are, as a result of that connection, forced to the surface by spirit. This work integrates traditional psychological theory and practice with the mystical realm. Psychology meets spirituality here. It is necessary to access Divine energies if we are to develop and grow in ways that have collective significance. No longer can we attempt to transform ourselves or our world without making a direct connection with the God energy.

The split I felt in the *epiphenomena* experience has disappeared. My intellect and soul have come together through this work.

A New Direction

As I conclude *Direct Connection* I find my mind wandering back to twenty years ago, the time when my journey began. I was a young married woman then, with two children and a new career before me. In my first job as a counselor, I worked with those who suffered from chronic mental illness. The innovative approach then employed was to medicate clients and to assist them behaviorally to function more effectively in the community. Today, this is the accepted approach for helping individuals with diagnoses of schizophrenia and bipolar disorder to live outside of psychiatric hospitals.

My journey over the last two decades has taken me far from where I started. I completed my doctoral studies in psychology, worked for ten years at a research and training organization where I assisted mental health professionals who work with the mentally ill, became a college professor, watched my son and daughter grow up and begin lives of their own, engaged in breathwork experiences, explored the mystical terrain, transformed my world view, traveled around the globe, and guided others on their own spiritual path.

Most recently my work has led me in a new direction, one that I hope to be actively engaged in for the next phase of my life. I am now working with the same population with which I began my career. These individuals are diagnosed as seriously mentally ill by the psychiatric establishment. At a partial hospitalization program I am working individually and in groups with persons who, for the most part, are labeled paranoid schizophrenic and are identified as chronic mentally ill patients. They are taking heavy doses of medication and have been hospitalized numerous times; they hear voices, see visions, and are unable to work or live independently without some form of supportive care.

What I have discovered is that *many of these individuals spontaneously made a direct connection years earlier.* Their connection with spirit was jolting and unmanageable. Strong energies passed through them and attached to their fears and unresolved psychological problems. As they made contact with their mystical roots, the dualistic energies of the Judeo-Christian tradition overwhelmed them with such images and visions as Christ and the devil. They had no knowledge of their true spiritual nature and received no support or guidance from any therapist or spiritual teacher. They were told by experts that their experiences were not real-that these events, the most profound and fearful experiences of their lives, had to be suppressed by medication, because what they described meant that they were mentally ill—that they were crazy.

Most of these individuals no longer speak to their doctors or therapists about their experiences. They have learned that when they do so they are regarded to be "sick," and their medication—which causes many unpleasant side effects—would be increased. I have learned from them that despite the efforts of psychiatry through medications and hospitalizations, their voices and visions continue. Some remain in constant fear, and they attribute all their "paranoid ideation," comprising negativity, feelings of being attacked, and the like, to dark energies. Others do better.

The Story of Frederick

Frederick was a member of one of the partial hospitalization programs where I worked. He was a tall man in his forties with deep lines in his face. He had short red hair, a full mustache, and bright blue eyes. One day when Frederick was seven years old, he was walking out of school and reported hearing a voice:

"Young Frederick, look up at the sky."

As he did so, he saw a brilliant, golden—white light surrounding Mary, who was holding baby Jesus. He then heard these words coming from Baby Jesus:

"I will be with you, young Frederick, for the rest of your life."

Frederick ran home to tell his mother. She took him to a psychiatrist. From that time forward he was put under the care of psychiatrists and was placed on heavy doses of antipsychotic medication. At no time was he allowed to mention his experience again. As an adult, Frederick lived for many years in supervised living facilities and attended partial hospitalization day programs.

When I asked Frederick if he was angry at the way his life had gone, he said:

"No, I used to be, but I no longer am. Jesus has grown up with me and stands beside me throughout my life. I have learned from Him that I must forgive all the people who know not what they do."

And when I asked Frederick how Jesus appeared to him now, I was struck by his response. He replied, "Jesus doesn't look as others describe Him. He has short red hair, a full mustache, and bright blue eyes."

I could not help but wonder if at some level Frederick seemed to understand that he was describing himself.

Unfortunately, Frederick's story culminated in tragedy. Approximately eight months after I terminated my work at Frederick's mental health facility, he died. In my opinion he paid the ultimate price for the gross inadequacies of the current system of psychiatric care.

Part of Frederick's mental health treatment was for him to live semi-independently in a residential facility in the community. In this facility he shared an apartment for eight years with another resident who participated in the same partial hospitalization day program that he did. In this type of residential setting, mental health staff are supposed to be available when needed. Frederick's roommate was Tom, a quiet man whom I never met but who was said to interact with Frederick in a friendly, peaceful manner.

One afternoon during the Christmas holiday season, Tom met with a staff psychiatrist at the partial hospitalization program. He told the psychiatrist, Dr. J., that he was concerned that he might harm someone. When Dr. J. questioned why Tom felt that way, he replied that Satan had come to him and asked him to be his follower. Tom further asserted that he was told he would be given great powers if he hurt someone. Dr. J. did not respond to what Tom said, nor did she pursue this discussion any further. Instead, she said that he needed to go to the psychiatric hospital to get his medication increased. She wrote him a prescription to present at the hospital and sent him on his way.

Tom did not go to the hospital. Instead, he went back to his apartment, feeling fear, panic, rage, and confusion. Upon entering the apartment, he saw Frederick, who in those few moments was perceived by Tom as his mortal enemy. Tom reached for a kitchen knife and plunged it into Frederick's heart.

Later that day Frederick was found dead, and Tom was taken to an institution for the criminally insane. Upon learning of this tragedy, I kept asking myself how such a horrible thing could have happened. Over time, I came to believe that both men were functioning dangerously out of balance. During this particular Christmas season, Frederick was probably making a literal identification with Jesus Christ and was out of contact with his own human vulnerabilities, fears, and personal shadow. Tom, on the other hand, felt no connection with the Light within himself. In their respective realities, they each were attached to totally opposite polarities.

What would have occurred if Dr. J. had let herself really *hear* Tom's words? Frederick was also her patient—she had known of his identification with Jesus, because she had written in his psychiatric records that he had "religious ideation" and "delusions of grandiosity." Had she really listened to each man's words with her heart, she might have treated them as human beings instead of diagnostic labels. Perhaps then she would have recognized that they were living in opposing extreme states and needed major assistance and compassion that necessitated more than increased medication. But she chose not to hear either man's soul crying out for help.

As I believe that Frederick and Tom were martyrs of their time, I am hopeful that their lives and deaths ultimately will not have been in vain. Professionals working in the mental health system must begin to really listen to what hundreds of thousands of patients in their care are *telling* them. They must understand that these patients need acknowledgment and guidance—not denial and neglect—in learning to cope with the realities of their experience.

As I continue to work with people who have psychiatric diagnoses, I am struck by the similarity of their spiritual perceptions and feelings. Whether Christians or Jews, most have experiences of

God, light and darkness, good and evil, Christ and the devil. So I have come to understand that much of what is attributed to serious mental illness in the West is in actuality a direct, though possibly distorted, mystical connection to one's Judeo-Christian roots. My two prophetic messages have guided me to this aspect of my work.

THE KINGDOM IS NOW

Over the last few years I have observed the development of clients committed to traveling the narrow path. They work together as a group as they engage in breathwork on a regular basis. Miracles that transcend time and space happen within the group and outside of it. Spiritual energy—reflecting worldwide happenings from the past and present—suffuse these people and lead to visions and synchronicities. The energy exchange results in deeply enhanced opportunities for transformation at individual and collective levels. Increasingly, I have learned that when people are alert and open to the spiritual lessons that the energy brings, they can make evolutionary leaps. Wherever there is light, there is darkness. The choices that each one of us makes individually or as a group have an important effect on the energy level of the world.

Themes pertaining to light and dark consistently emerge during breathwork for members of the group with whom I work. Often these themes manifest in Christ Consciousness, swastika images, the Holocaust, and Divine Mother energy. Our group is one of many now forming worldwide to learn the spiritual truths for our time.

A woman of Protestant Celtic roots brought to our last intensive workshop a gold menorah spattered with red paint and covered with nails. It had been a gift to her daughter, who had recently married a Jewish man. Did this menorah represent the Holocaust or Christ's crucifixion? Another person in our group, of Jewish background, frequently dies in a boxcar taking him to the camps. Although born Jewish, he regards Jesus as his spiritual teacher and guide. Recently I visited two residents at a half-way house in Philadelphia. Both women, diagnosed schizophrenic, were long-term patients. The walls of both their apartments were covered with their artwork. The drawings of the older woman, an African American, included the Christian cross, the Jewish star, and the words "Holy, Holy." The drawings of the other woman, Jewish American, included pictures of Jesus and swastikas.

I was born in the middle of World War II when Hitler was walking the earth. As we approach the third millennium, it is time for us who have Judeo-Christian spiritual roots to turn away from this phase of our darkness and look toward the Light, the New Age, the Kingdom of God on earth. I believe that this is why these themes emerge for me, for my clients, and for others in the Western part of the world who have made the direct connection.

Benedict T. Viviano, a professor of the New Testament at the École Biblique, Jerusalem, and Dean of Studies at the Ecumenical Research Institute, Tantur, wrote in the introduction to his book *The Kingdom of God* in History:

> *It early became obvious to me that the central theme of the preaching of the historical Jesus of Nazareth was the near approach of the kingdom of God. Yet to my amazement, this theme played hardly any role in the systematic theology I had been taught in the seminary. Upon further investigation, I realized that this theme had in many ways been largely ignored in the theology and spirituality and liturgy of the Church in the past two thousand years and, when not*

ignored, often distorted beyond recognition. How could this be? In a word, the kingdom was explosive power, if only it was fully understood. (page 9)

When Jesus' disciples persisted in looking for the Kingdom in time, asking, "When will the Kingdom come?" Jesus answered:

It will not come by waiting for it. It will not be a manner of saying "here it is or there it is." Rather, the Kingdom of the Father is spread out upon the earth, and men do not see it.

Jesus understood the Kingdom to be a state of being, a transformed consciousness, a radical change of attitude. Entering it means we are being taken care of, at every moment. It is always here. All spiritual teachers, in all the great religious traditions, have come to experience living in the present as the only reality.

No longer am I split between the old paradigm and the new. The Kingdom is now—the new has eventuated. As spiritual energy intensifies around the globe, people who resist will grasp tightly to old constraints and limitations. Those of us who make the direct connection must keep moving forward. We must incorporate the truth by turning away from the darkness and toward the Light. Through our choices we will awaken others to their true Divine nature and, in so doing, assist them to let go of old values based on fear, dishonesty, violence, and power.

We were born at this time in evolutionary history to lead others to the Kingdom on earth. If we live the truth of what we now know, others will begin to remember what they temporarily forgot. Our potential is unlimited, and we are an integral part of eternity.

Appendix
Chapter Notes

Preface and Introduction

In *Hero with a Thousand Faces*, Joseph Campbell points out the underlying similarities of all religions and mythologies. He views "the hero's journey" as a basic truth that keeps playing out throughout the history of humanity. The third printing of this book is part of the Bollingen Series XVII, Princeton University Press, 1973.

St. Martin's quotation is found in *Mysticism* by Evelyn Underhill, p. 80, Doubleday, New York, 1990. St. Martin's original text is *Man: His True Nature*, translated by E.B. Penny, London, 1864.

The Universe and Dr. Einstein is a clear and readable book on Einstein's theories written by Lincoln Barnett and published by Bantam Books, New York, 1948, with a foreword by Albert Einstein. The quotation in my Introduction is taken from Chapter 15 of the second revised edition of Barnett's book printed in 1957.

CHAPTER 1 A New Way of Working

John Nelson describes "spiritual ground" as a radically expanded view of consciousness in *Healing the Split: Integrating Spirit into our Understanding of the Mentally Ill*, New York, SUNY Press, 1994.

In Myths to Live By (1972) Joseph Campbell discusses the ways in which schizophrenia parallels the Hero's Journey. (New York, Viking Press p. 216).

The DSM IV is the Diagnostic and Statistical Manual of Mental Disorders, published by the American Psychiatric Association in Washington, D.C. (1994).

Joseph Campbell discusses the significance of "following one's bliss" in *The Power of Myth*, p. 92, Doubleday, New York, 1988 and in *An Open Life*, p. 18, Carson Publications, New York, 1988.

Between Two Worlds, written by psychologist Frederick Weidmann, is a statement that can be summed in his words: "when clinical psychology rejects the soul, then clinical psychology loses its ability to heal." Weidmann acknowledges that the school of Transpersonal psychology is an approach that comes the closest to resolving the problem, but at the same time voices major criticism against it. Between Two Worlds was published in 1986 by the Theosophical Publishing House, Wheaton, IA.

Marilyn Ferguson wrote the very popular book *The Aquarian Conspiracy: Personal and Social Transformation* in the 1980's, published by Tarcher, Los Angeles in 1980. It is a commentary on our times with recommendations for change.

CHAPTER 2 In the Beginning

Walter and Mary Jo Uphoff in *New Psychic Frontiers* (Minneapolis: Bolger Publications 1980) present an overview of parapsychology in a straightforward manner. The Uphoffs also identify various mediums who have been well known and describe their major characteristics on page 14.

Scholars presenting significant perspectives in the field of parapsychology include Anthony Flew, who edited *Advances in Parapsychological Research* (New York: Prometheus Books, 1987). Also Laurance LeShahn in *The Medium, the Mystic and the Physicist* (New York: Viking Press, 1974) and *Alternate Realities* (New York: M. Evans and Co., 1976) discusses a general theory of the paranormal and how this relates to different levels of consciousness. In addition, Stanley Krippner has edited a series of books, *Advances in Parapsychological Research* (Jefferson, N.C., McFarland and Co., 1984) from an academic and scientific approach.

Hypnagogic states and other out-of-body and altered states of consciousness are investigated by psychoanalysts Glen Gabbard and Stuart Twemlow in *With the Eyes of the Mind* (New York: Praeger, 1984). Trained in the scientific method, they explore aspects of the consciousness movement from psychoanalytic, neurophysiological, and philosophical perspectives.

Gabbard and Twemlow also discuss the motor paralysis found in hypnagogic states, as does Steven LaBerge. LaBerge writes about the power of being awake and aware in your dreams in *Lucid Dreaming* (Los Angeles: Tarcher, 1985). Data culled from his five-year study at the Stanford University Sleep Research Center are discussed in terms of the extraordinary potentialities of the human mind. Gabbard and Twemlow have also done extensive out-of-body research at the Menninger Clinic in Topeka, Kansas.

Berthold Schwartz presents an up-to-date scientific evaluation of psychic phenomena that he has identified in psychiatry and everyday life. His book *Psychic-Nexus* was published in New York by Van Nostrand Reinhold Co. in 1980.

David Bohm, one of the outstanding physicists in the world today, is recognized for his groundbreaking work in New Physics. Bohm's classic book *Wholeness and the Implicate Order* was published in London by Routledge and Kegan Paul in 1980.

Wilder Penfield questioned the results of his life's work as a neurologist in *The Mystery of the Mind*, Princeton University Press, 1976.

Thomas Kuhn in *The Structure of Scientific Revolutions*, University of Chicago Press, 2nd edition, 1962, challenges scientific research: "a strenuous and devoted effort to force nature into the conceptual boxes supplied by professional education."

Charles Tart, a leader in the investigation of altered states of consciousness, has likened our normal waking state of consciousness to being asleep in comparison to other states of awareness we might attain. His definition of an altered state of consciousness is found in *Science Journal*, Vol. 176, p. 1203-10, 1972. Recent books he has written are *Altered States of Consciousness and Waking Up*.

In *Revision: The Journal of Consciousness and Change* (Winter/Spring

1986, Vol. 8, No. 2) Christina and Stanislav Grof identify different levels of consciousness: "Spiritual Emergency: The Understanding and Treatment of Transpersonal Crises."

The Archetypes and the Collective Unconscious by C.J. Jung discusses the theoretiocal basis of the collective unconscious and it's relationship to individuation. Published by Princeton University Press, it is part of Bollinger Series II, 1969.

The Future of the Body by Michael Murphy was published by Tarcher, Inc., Los Angeles, in 1992. Murphy describes exceptional functioning of body, mind, and spirit and sees this as evidence of future evolutionary development.

The predictions stated by Nostradamus were written by E. Cheetam in *The Man Who Saw Tomorrow: The Prophecies of Nostradamus* (New York: Berkeley Books, 1973).

CHAPTER 3 The Art of Dying

Raymond Moody, Jr., a psychiatrist, in *Life After Life* (Atlanta: Mockingbird Books, 1975) interviews many people who have had similar mystical experiences in the moments that they were technically dead. He coined the term "near-death experience" (NDE) to describe such encounters with death. This book became a national bestseller, and millions of near-death experiencers felt much relief when they could read about experiences that they had undergone but were afraid to discuss for fear that people would think they were crazy.

My experiences, which have seemed to parallel those near-death experiences, have included out-of-body experiences, seeing and being part of a white light, feeling a sense of love in an altered state that goes beyond anything that can be felt in our ordinary state of consciousness, and having people who have died communicate with me. The near-death experience has been described effectively in *Life at Death* by Kenneth Ring (New York: Coward McCann and Geoghegan Gan, 1980).

Kenneth Ring moved beyond his earlier near-death studies and describes characteristics of people having psychospiritual experiences in his two books, *Heading Toward Omega* (William Morrow Co., 1984) and *The Omega Project* (William Morrow Co., 1992).

Kimberly Clark Sharp discusses her spiritual journey after her near-death experience in *After the Light*, published by William Morrow in 1995.

Full Circle by Barbara Harris and Lionel C. Bascom (New York: Pocket Books, 1990) tells of her NDE and the implications its aftereffects have had on her life. In *Spiritual Awakenings* (by Barbara Harris Whitfield, Health Communications, Inc., 1995), she discusses in-depth how her NDE was a catalyst for a deep transformational process.

Barbara Harris also describes aspects of her NDE in an article in *McCall's* magazine in February 1988. This article, "The Near-Death Experience," written by Amy Sunshine Genova, discusses research, varying theoretical perspectives, and case examples.

Yvonne Kason, M.D., describes the ways in which NDEs and other extraordinary experiences change ordinary lives in *A Farther Shore* (Harper Collins, 1994).

Beyond Death by Stanislav and Christina Grof (London: Thames and Hudson, 1980) is a beautiful book that explores the concepts of an afterlife in many religions and cultures.

The Book of the Dead by Budge, E.A. Wallis (New York: University Books, 1960) explores Egyptian death-rebirth rituals. Also Evans-Wentz, W.E. in *The Tibetan Book of the Dead* (London: Oxford University Press, 1957), reviews, from the Tibetan perspective, each phase that persons who have died will go through as they begin their afterlife spiritual journey.

Ian Stevenson, a psychiatrist at the University of Virginia, has devoted more than thirty years of his career to the study of reincarnation. He has spent much time in India doing research into this phenomenon; in his first major book, he documented case histories of people who give evidence of their past lives. This book, *Twenty Cases Suggestive of Reincarnation* (Charlottesville: University Press of Virginia, 1966) is considered a classic in the field.

The following books are a small sample of works that discuss certain principles that are related to after-death existence. "Karma," one of these principles, is a Sanskrit word that has entered the English vocabulary. It signifies the principle of moral causation by which man reaps as he sows; it denotes the law of moral causation that links man to the cycle of repeated incarnation in the material world or in superphysical realms. Swami Muktananda discussed these issues in several of his works: *Plays of Consciousness* (South Fallsburg, NY: Syda Foundation, 1971), *Kundalini* (Syda

Foundation, 1979), and *Meditate* (Syda Foundation, 1980); Krishnamurti also discussed these perspectives in *The Awakening of Intelligence* (San Francisco: Harper and Row, 1973). Three other books of interest that discuss these themes from a cross-cultural perspective are: *Christianity Meets Buddhism* by Heinrich Dumoulin S.J. (LaSalle, Illinois: Open Court Publishing Co., 1974); *Mysticism, East and West* by Rudolf Otto (reprinted by Theosophical Society in America, 1987); and *The Atman Project* by Ken Wilber (Theosophical Publishing House, U.S.A., 1980).

Easy Death by DaFree John is a spiritual text and an extended discourse on death itself. DaFree John, whose original name was Franklin Albert Jones, has been proclaimed a fully realized Western adept. An *adept* is considered an Enlightened being who has been able to transcend the universal law of karma and hence the suffering in all the dimensions of manifest existence.

CHAPTER 4 A Priest and the Tree of Life

In Beyond the Brain (New York: State University of New York Press, 1985) Stanislav Grof condensed into a single volume almost thirty years of research on non-ordinary states of consciousness induced by psychedelic drugs and a variety of non-pharmacological methods.

John Weir Perry describes the nature of spirit in relation to breath in "Spiritual Emergence and Renewal," in *Revision*, Vol. 8, No. 2, 1986.

Books discussing Kundalini from both Western and Eastern interpretations include *Kundalini, The Secret of Life*, by Swami Muktananda (South Fallsburg, NY: Syda Foundation, 1979); *The*

Kundalini Experience by Lee Sannella (Lower Lake, California: Integral Publishing, 1987); *Kundalini for the New Age* edited by Gene Kieffer (New York: Bantam Books, 1988); *Kundalini Yoga for the West* by S. Radha (Spokane, Washington: Timeless Books, 1978); *Kundalini* by L. Silburn (Albany, NY: SUNY, 1988); *The Serpent Power* by J. Woodroofe (Ganesh, India: 1974).

Gopi Krishna, a modern-day sage and self-taught prophet from India, discusses his own Kundalini awakening, which lasted for many years, and his perspectives on this phenomenon in *The Biological Basis of Religious and Genius* (New York: Harper and Row, 1972); *The Wonder of the Brain* (Ontario, Canada: F.I.N.D. Research Trust, 1987); and *Kundalini, The Evolutionary Energy in Man* (Boston: Shambhala, 1985).

Proceedings from the Academy of Religion and Psychical Research, Thirteenth Annual Conference on Kundalini; *Biological Basis of Religion and Genius,* included a comprehensive review by John White on *Kundalini, Evolution and Enlightenment* (Black Mountain, NC: 1988).

Gene Kieffer's paper *Soma and the Shifting Paradigm* was also presented at the conference and is part of the proceedings.

Bonnie Greenwald discusses characteristics and patterns exhibited in persons experiencing Kundalini awakening in her paper *Kundalini: Understanding and Nurturing Energy Consciousness and the Emergent Self,* also in the proceedings.

CHAPTER 5 Shamanism and Spiritual Initiation

Angeles Arrien, trained as a shaman in the Basque culture, combines her training and experience with her work as an anthropologist. In "Four Basic Archetypal Ways Found in Shamanic Traditions" (*Revision: The Journal of Consciousness and Change*, Fall, 1990, Vol. 13, No. 2), Arrien describes in detail the characteristics and tasks inherent in the shaman as healer, warrior, adventurer or teacher.

Joseph Campbell gives us historical and mythological evidence of the roots of Shamanism in *The Way of the Animal Powers (Part 1: Mythologies of the Primitive Hunters and Gatherers and Part 2: Mythologies of the Great Hunt)* (Philadelphia: Harper and Row, 1988).

Jeanne Achterberg describes characteristics of Shamanism and relates these to modern medicine in *Imagery in Healing* (Boston: Shambhala, 1985).

The Herder Symbol Dictionary, translated from "Herder Lexikon Symbole" by Boris Matthews, describes over 1000 symbols from art, archeology, mythology, literature, and religion (Wilmette, IL: Chiron, 1986).

Major alchemical texts are *Crowns of Nature* by Barchusen, *The Twelve Keys of Basil Valentine,* and *Bibliotheca Chenuca Curiosa* (1702). A modern text by Johannes Fabricius is *Alchemy: The Medieval Alchemists and Their Royal Art* (Copenhagen: Rosenkilde and Bogger, 1976)

Carl Jung wrote *Psychology and Alchemy* in 1944. It can be found in Jung's Collected Works (Princeton, NJ: Princeton University Press, 1988-Bollingen Series XX).

Roger Walsh in *The Spirit of Shamanism* (Los Angeles: Tarcher, 1990) has provided a comprehensive, absorbing account of Shamanism. This book has been recognized as a major step toward the understanding of Shamanism.

The Way of the Shaman by Michael Harner (New York: Bantam Books, 1980) is a classic introductory text for those hoping to learn Shamanic techniques.

In recent years several books have been written on the topic of Shamanism for the contemporary non-tribal student who demonstrates interest in Shamanic techniques. Joan Halifax's *Shamanic Voices* (New York: E. P. Dutton, 1979) and *Shaman: The Wounded Healer* (London: Thames and Hudson, 1982) provide a comprehensive perspective. Other books of timely interest include: *Birth of a Modern Shaman* by Cynthia Bend and Tayja Wiger (St. Paul, Minn: Llewelyn Publications, 1988); *The Realms of Healing* by Stanley Krippner and Alberto Villoldo (Berkeley, CA: Celestial Arts, 1976); *Shaman's Path: Healing, Personal Growth and Empowerment* by G. Doore (Boston: Shambhala, 1988). There is also a journal for those interested in this topic. It is called *Shaman's Drum* and is published by the Cross-Cultural Shamanism Network, Berkeley, CA.

CHAPTER 6 Beyond Time and Space

Numerous books on the collective unconscious have been written by Jung and others. Relevant books by Jung include *Analytical*

Psychology: Its Theory and Practice. The Tavistock Lectures (New York: Random House, Vintage Books, 1968); *On the Nature of the Psyche* in Collected Works, Vol. 8, (Princeton, NJ: Bollingen Series XX, Princeton University Press, 1954); *The Psychogenesis of Mental Disease* (Princeton: Princeton University Press, 1960); *Symbols of Transformation*, (Princeton, NJ: Bollingen Series XX, Princeton University Press, 1956); *Memories, Dreams, Reflections* (New York: Random House, Vintage Books, 1989). Joseph Campbell reviewed Jung's work in *The Portable Jung* (New York: Penguin Books, 1976), and Stephan Hoeller describes Jung as a mystic in *The Gnostic Jung and the Seven Sermons to the Dead* (Wheaton, IL: The Theosophical Publishing House, 1982). Also, F. David Peat reviews Jung and some of his concepts in *Synchronicity: The Bridge Between Matter and Mind* (New York: Bantam Books, 1987).

Jung describes the various archetypes of the collective unconscious in *The Archetypes and the Collective Unconscious* (Princeton, NJ: Bollingen Series XX, Princeton University Press, 1969).

Various meanings of the crab are found in the *Woman's Dictionary of Symbols and Sacred Objects* by Barbara G. Walker (San Francisco: Harper & Row, 1988) as well as in *The Herder Symbol Dictionary*, translated by Boris Matthews (Wilmette, IL: Chiron Publishers, 1988).

Jung discusses synchronicity in *Synchronicity: An Acausal Connecting Principle* (Collected Works, Vol. 8, Princeton, NJ: Bollingen Series XX, Princeton University Press).

More detailed analysis of the relationship between physics and mysticism is described in *Wholeness and the Implicate Order* by David

Bohm (London: Routledge and Kegan Paul, 1980) and in *No Boundary* by Ken Wilber (Boston and London: Shambhala Press, 1985).

Jesus, A New Vision, by Marcus Borg, looks at Jesus from a historical perspective. Published by Harper San Francisco in 1987, it is acknowledged as providing a fresh and authentic look at Jesus.

I.P. Couliano in his book *Out of This World* (Boston: Shambhala Press, 1991) made reference to Einstein's thoughts. This book takes the reader on a journey that examines the phenomena of visionary experiences in many cultures.

Charles Hinton's perspectives on a fourth dimension are also discussed in *Out of This World*. Couliano makes reference to Rudy Rucker's introduction to *Speculations on the Fourth Dimension: Selected Writings Outside Charles H. Hinton*. This book, edited by Rucker, was published by Dover in New York, 1980.

Couliano also cites Paul Davis' book *Superforce: The Search for a Grand Unified Theory of Nature* (New York: Simon and Schuster, 1984) as a source for important new perspectives in physics.

The 5th Dimension, by Sheila Peterson-Lowary, is one source that identifies how we are living in a time that goes beyond the 4th dimension. This book was published by Simon and Schuster in 1988.

The Nothingness Beyond God by Robert E. Carter is an introduction to the philosophy of Nishida Kitaro. Kitaro is considered a great 20th-century Japanese philosopher who interpreted Western philosophy in the context of the Japanese language and culture. His goal was the ultimate synthesis of Eastern and Western thoughts. His book was published by Paragon House, New York in 1989.

Since my personal extraterrestrial experiences, I have read some provocative and thoroughly documented books on the subject. The following ones may be of interest to the reader: *The Starseed Transmissions* by Ken Carey (Santa Fe, NM: Bear and Co., 1982); also by Carey, *Starseed, The Third Millennium* (San Francisco: Harper 1991); *Angels and Aliens: UFOs and the Mythic Imagination* by Keith Thompson (Reading, Mass: Addison-Wesley, 1991); *The Omega Project* by Kenneth Ring (New York: William Morrow and Co., 1992).

Abduction by John Mack reviews case histories of people reporting human encounters with aliens. Published by Charles Scribner, NY, 1994.

CHAPTER 7 Identity Crisis: Christian Mysticism

In *The Bleeding Mind* Ian Wilson investigates the phenomenon of stigmata. He questions whether they are divinely bestowed replications of the actual wounds of Jesus or whether they result from a strange mental process yet to be understood. The book was published by Weidenfeld and Nicholson, London, 1988.

Oliver Davies, a writer, researcher, and translator living in Wales, writes about Christian mysticism of Northern Europe in the Middle Ages. His book, *God Within: The Mystical Tradition of Northern Europe*, discusses the general context of the medieval church's spirituality. He discusses such mystics as Jan van Ruusbroec, Johannes Tauler, Henry Suso, and Walter Hilton and emphasizes how the North European tradition is based on a sense of inwardness. This book was published by Paulist Press, New York and New Jersey, in 1988.

The quotation by St. Theresa is found on p. 292 in *Mysticism* by Evelyn Underhill. This book, published by Doubleday, New York, in 1990, was originally published in London in 1911. It is considered the preeminent study in the nature and development of spiritual consciousness. It is the classic in its field and is thoroughly documented with material drawn from such great mystics as St. Theresa of Avila, Meister Eckhart, St. John of the Cross, William Blake and many others.

The Spirit of Shamanism, written by Roger Walsh in 1990, was referred to earlier in Chapter 5. There it was referenced as an important work on Shamanism. Its relevance here is in the comparison that Walsh made between the shaman and the Christian mystic.

CHAPTER 8 Process That Never Ends

The Herder Symbol Dictionary, translated by Boris Matthews, contains reviews of various interpretations of fire. Published by Chiron, Wilmette, IL, 1988.

Evelyn Underhill in *Mysticism* (pp. 193-4) reviewed several English mystics' perspectives on their experience of fire. She quotes Richard Rolle, author of The Fire of Love; Walter Hilton, author of *Scale of Perfection*; the unknown author of the little classic *The Cloud of Unknowing*, and Madeleine Seimer in *Coinvertie et Mystique*.

Julian of Norwich, translated by Brendan Doyle, is a book of meditations written by a female English mystic in 1373. When Julian was thirty and a half years old, she reported seeing mystical visions and recorded the content of these revelations in a text titled *A Book of Showings*. At a later time in her life she became an anchoress attached to the Church of St. Julian at Norwich and then took the name of this patron saint. Julian's vision focusing on "God-with-in-us" was the basis of her meditations. This book was published by Bear and Co. in Santa Fe, New Mexico, in 1983.

The Dark Face of Reality by Martin Israel, a priest in the Church of England as well as a practicing physician, was published by Morehouse-Barlow, in Wilton, Connecticut, in 1989. Israel's focus is the recognition of our potential for evil, on both personal and societal levels, as a part of our aspiration to goodness. Israel shows potential good emerging from the terrible events of the twentieth century. He emphasizes the integration of light and darkness.

In Mysticism by Evelyn Underhill one can read theoretical information pertaining to spiritual consciousness that has been documented cross-culturally through time. While some information is given regarding Eastern mysticism, her emphasis is on Christian mystical tradition.

CHAPTER 9 Unitive Experience

Fritjof Capra reconciles Eastern philosophy and spiritual traditions with Western science in *The Tao of Physics* (New York: Bantam Books, 1977). This book presents a thorough overview of differing Eastern spiritual traditions.

Sogyal Rinpoche was born in Tibet and was raised by one of the most revered spiritual masters of this century, Jamyang Khyentse Chokyi Ladro. Rinpoche is an authority on the teachings associated with the *Tibetan Book of the Dead*. In his book *The Tibetan Book of Living and Dying* (Harper San Francisco, 1992) he transmits the accumulated insights of centuries of Tibetan Buddhism.

The Tibetan Book of the Dead, translated by W.E. Evans Wentz, was published by Oxford University Press in London in 1957. This book is based on a secret oral tradition and was first put into its written form in the eighth century A.D. by Padma Sambhava, who introduced Buddhism to Tibet. It is a guide through the states between death and rebirth.

Rudolf Otto in *Mysticism East and West* compares the two principal classic types of Eastern and Western mystical experience. It was first published by Macmillan Co. in 1932, and later by Quest, Wheaton, IL, in 1987.

Thomas Merton, one of the great modern scholars and theologians of the 20th century, wrote *Mystics and Zen Masters*. In it he examined the great contemplative tradition of the East and West. The first edition of this book was published in 1967, and the fifth edition in 1989 by The Noonday Press, New York.

Michael Murphy, author of the *Future of the Body*, paints a broad picture of the possibilities of further evolutionary development of human attributes.

Play of Consciousness is the spiritual autobiography of Swami Muktananda. One of his important achievements as a teacher was to make clear that a fully realized Master is one who has discovered in his own experience the origin of all philosophies, whether it be Hinduism, Christianity, Judaism, or Islam. It was published by Syda Foundation, South Fallsburg, New York, 1971.

Autobiography of a Yogi by Parmanhansa Yogananda has become a classic in its field, revealing the scientific foundation underlying the great religious paths of both East and West. It has been translated into eighteen languages. It was published by Self-Realization Fellowship, Los Angeles, CA, in 1974 and reissued in 1981 and 1990. The author initially, self-published the book in 1946.

The Starseed Transmissions by Ken Carey has been described as the modern classic of intuitive knowledge that offers a startling new view of human spiritual evolution. It was published by Harper San Francisco in 1982.

CHAPTER 10 The Divine Feminine

Encountering Mary (New York: Avon Books, 1991) by Sandra L. Zindars-Swartzy provides detailed accounts of modern Marian apparitions that have been reported around the world. It is an objective, scrupulously researched study of what has been identified by some as an extraordinary socioreligious phenomenon with significant consequences for our civilization and our future.

Hidden Journey (New York: Arkana Books, 1991) by Andrew Harvey is a beautifully written and honest story of Harvey's spiritual awakening through the healing presence of the Divine Mother. Harvey, a rationalist atheist, made a total transformation following his encounter with Mother Mira, an eighteen-year-old Indian woman, who is the embodiment of the Divine Mother.

A description of a guru is discussed in *InterCommunion* by Sondra Ray, published by Celestial Arts, Berkeley, CA, 1990, and in *Babaji, Shri Haidakhan Wale Baba* by Gunnel Minett, p. 8.

In *Daughters of the Goddess: The Women Saints of India*, Linda Johnsen discusses the personal and spiritual lives of India's women of spirit. It was published by Yes International Publishers, St. Paul, MN, in 1994.

Mary's role as spiritual mother for the impoverished of the world is discussed in *Mary: Mother of God, Mother of the Poor* by J. Gebra and M. Bingeman (translated by P. Berrman), Arbis Books, NY, 1989.

In *Imitation of Mary*, written by Alexandre Joseph de Rouville in France in 1768, the author follows the Blessed Virgin through the different mysteries and circumstances of her life, from her Immaculate Conception to her Assumption into heaven. The book was edited and translated by Matthew J. O'Connell and published by Catholic Book Publishing Co. in New York, 1985.

The Mother of the Savior and Our Interior Life by Fr. Reginald Garrigon-Langrance and translated by Fr. Bernard J. Kelly was published by Tan Publishers, Illinois, 1948. This book explores every aspect of the role of Mary, her intercession for the human race and peace of the world.

An exploration drawing on religious traditions, cultures, and archaeological sources from around the world, throughout the ages, that focuses on the Goddess religion, *The Great Cosmic Mother: Rediscovering the Religion of the Earth* by M. Sjoo and B. Mor was published by Harper and Row, San Francisco, CA, 1975.

Two popular books that discuss Mary's messages to the world in the twentieth century are *Alone of All Her Sex* by Marina Warner (New York: Vintage Books, 1983) and *Mary's Message to the World* by Annie Kirkwood (CA: Blue Dolphin, 1991).

Ephesus, translated by Hayriye Buyan, was printed by Keskin Color Kartpostalcilik, Ltd. in 1994. It is a guidebook for tourists that describes the history and story of the Virgin Mary's house in Ephesus, Turkey.

CHAPTER 11 Healing at Auschwitz: The Wall Came Down

The Mother of the Savior and Our Interior Life has been described by its translator (Fr. Bernard J. Kelly) as a work that will inflame hearts and enlighten minds. It has also been called the finest summation of the Catholic church's teaching about the Mother of God. Written by Fr. Reginald Garrigon-Lagrange in 1941, it was republished by Tan Books, Rockford, IL, in 1993.

The *1963 National Catholic Almanac*, edited by Felician A. Foy, O.F.M., St. Andrew's Guild, Patterson, NJ, distributed by Doubleday, Garden City, NY, 1963.

The *Secrets of the Rosary* by St. Louis De Montfort; translated by Mary Barbour, T.O.P., Montfort Publications, NY, distributed by Tan Books, Rockford, IL, 1954.

CHAPTER 12 Good and Evil

Jesus, A New Vision, by Marcus J. Borg was published by Harper San Francisco, 1987. It presents in a scholarly way what the historical Jesus was like, what he taught, and what his mission was about. It describes nondogmatically Jesus as a figure of history before his death.

The Gospel According to Jesus is a book focusing on the life and teachings of Jesus by scholar and translator Stephen Mitchell. While the Gospels according to Mark, Matthew, Luke, and John are to a large extent teachings about Jesus, Mitchell compiled a Gospel that is the teaching of Jesus. He has retained only the authentic sayings and doings of Jesus, and has omitted the passages added by the early church. Gone are the passages which call Jesus the son of God, in contrast to the authentic Jesus' teaching that all people can become sons or daughters of God, and they become like God—generous, compassionate, impartial, serene. What remains is an image of Jesus as a real person and as a great spiritual teacher. Mitchell draws parallels between Jesus' teachings and the Buddhist, Hindu, Taoist, Sufi, and Jewish traditions. This book was published by Harper Collins in 1991.

Matthew Fox, in *The Coming of the Cosmic Christ* applies Jesus' teachings to the healing of the earth and the birth of a global renaissance. Published by Harper and Row in San Francisco, 1988.

Emanuel Swedenborg's *Heaven and Hell* was first published in Latin in London in 1758. Its 58th printing, translated by George Dole, was published by the Swedenborg Foundation, NY, 1990. Swedenborg, considered the West's most remarkable theologian and philosopher, reveals a comprehensive description of life hereafter—based on his experiences in the spiritual realm.

In Symbols of Transformation Carl Jung discusses the process of individuation and transformation. Published by Princeton University Press, Bollingen Series XX, 1956.

M. Scott Peck, the psychiatrist who wrote *People of the Lie*, integrates the insights of psychiatry with those of religion. It examines, through case studies, the problem of human evil. It was published by Simon and Schuster in 1983.

In Healing the Child Within: Discovery & Recovery for Adult Children of Dysfunctional Families, Charles Whitfield describes the pain underlying negativity found in dysfunctional families (Health Communications, 1987).

Related books on the problem of human evil include *The Devil's Bride: Exorcism Past and Present and Possession and Exorcism*, both by Martin Ebon, Colin Smyth Publishers, England; *The Dark Face of Reality* by Martin Israel, Morehouse-Barlow Publishers; *Hostage to the Devil* by Malachi Martin, Bantam Books; *The Pain of Christ and the Sorrow of God* by Gerald Vann, Aquin Press; *Good and Evil* by Martin Buber, Scribner.

Evil, the Shadow Side of Reality, by John Sanford, discusses the problem of evil from insights obtained from psychology, mythology, literature, philosophy, and Christianity. Published by Crossroad, NY, 1990.

Hamlet's statement to Rosencrantz, Hamlet, Act II, Scene 2, line 259, written by William Shakespeare. "There is nothing either good or bad, but thinking makes it so."

William McNamara, O.C.D., is a monk and a Roman Catholic priest. He is the author of *The Human Adventure* (1974), *Mystical Passion* (1977), and *Christian Mysticism* (1981), republished as a trilogy by Amity House in 1987. Other works include *The Art of Being*

Human (1967), now out of print, and *Earthy Mysticism* (1983). He founded the Spiritual Life Institute of America, a small monastic community of men and women, Roman Catholic in origin and universal in outreach. It has two locations: Cresstone, Colorado, and Kemptville, Nova Scotia, Canada. All of his publications are available from the Spiritual Life Institute. His ideas in this book come primarily from his chapter "Psychology and the Christian Mystical Tradition" cited in *Transpersonal Psychologies: Perspectives on the Mind from Seven Great Spiritual Traditions*, edited by Charles T. Tart.

Charles T. Tart, author of *Waking Up and Altered States of Consciousness*, is editor of *Transpersonal Psychologies: Perspectives on the Mind from Seven Great Spiritual Traditions*, published by Harper and Row, San Francisco, 1975.

Father McNamara quotes Dr. Gregory Zilboorg, a psychologist and one of America's foremost historians and philosophers of medicine: "While psychology can throw a great deal of psychological light on religious experience, and religious faith may enrich one's psychological functioning, psychology as a scientific discipline can shed no light whatsoever on the relations between man and God."

H. Bars, discusses Christian mystical tradition in "Maritain's Contributions to an Understanding of Mystical Experience," in J. Evans, editor, *Jacques Maritain: The Man and His Achievement*, published in New York by Sheed and Word, 1963.

CHAPTER 13 Garden of the Soul

The Garden of the Soul contains public and private devotions of most frequent use. It was published in London by Burns, Oates and

Washbourne Ltd. There is no publishing date, but it appears to have been published around 1920.

Insight Guides—Indonesia, edited by Eric Dey and published by Houghton Mifflin Co., 1994, provides the visitor to Indonesia with important facts about the many Indonesian islands. This information is historical, religious, cultural, and demographic.

The Sufi treatise, *The Guide of the Peace and the Love to the Way of Allah*, Siddi Muhammad Press, 1994, provides an in-depth guide to Sufi tradition. Written by Siddi S. Muhammad al-Jamal ar-Rifani as-Shadihili.

CHAPTER 14 Transformation of Consciousness

Benedict T. Viviano, O.P., wrote *The Kingdom of God in History*. It was published by Michael Glazier, Inc., Wilmington, DE, 1988.

Godseed: The Journey of Christ by Jean Houston presents the story of Christ through individual and group exercise, including creative arts, dance, ceremony, and drama. She draws from interdisciplinary schools in her presentation. *Godseed* was published by Quest Books, Wheaton, IL, in 1992. It was originally published by Amity Press in 1988.

Index

Alchemy 82, 83
Allah 96, 144
Alphabet 102
Armageddon 127, 128, 129
Aum 141, 142
Auschwitz 171, 172, 175
Awakening of the Self 131

Berlin Wall 171, 172, 175
Bioplasm 71
Bipolar Disorder 12, 207
Blessed Mother 150
Blue Light 117, 118
Blue Mosque 168
Brahman IX, 139, 140, 142, 144
Buchenwald 173
Buddha IX, 89, 139, 144, 205
Buddhism 90

Campbell, Joseph VII, 13
Carey, Ken 142, 143
Cartesian Newtonian Model
  of the Universe 92
Catholic 68, 111, 113, 148, 151, 154,
  160-164, 167, 169, 173, 175, 178,
  205
Chakras 70
Chartes 100
Chi 71

Christ Consciousness IX, 18, 141, 142,
  205, 212
Christian 39, 56, 70, 89-91, 96, 99, 106,
  109, 111, 116, 120, 125, 127, 141,
  142, 144, 152, 170, 176, 195, 205,
  211, 212, 213
Christ, Jesus 17, 18, 111, 113, 117,
125,
  143, 150, 152, 154, 162, 169, 169,
  170, 175, 176, 178, 186-188, 205,
  209, 211-214
Clairaudience 31
Collective unconscious 87, 89, 90-92,
  97, 204
Cord rosary 162-164, 169, 170, 175,
  176
Cosmic mother 148
Crab 91
Crucifixion 18, 100, 111, 113, 213

Darkness 8, 129, 151, 178, 183-186,
  188, 189, 191, 205, 208, 212, 213
Dark night of the soul 132
Davies, Oliver 116
Death 41-43, 46, 50-53, 56, 57, 90,
114,
  122, 195, 204
Death-rebirth process 73, 113, 194, 199
Delusions of grandiosity 211
Diagnostic and Statistical Manual

(DSM IV) 14
Diego, Juan 167
Dionyous 89
Divine feminine 148
Divine wind 75, 77
Doyle, Brandon 128

Eckhart, Meister 144
Ego death 57, 72, 73, 131
Einstein, Albert X, 92, 98
Ephesus 167, 168
Epiphenomena 32-35, 76, 93, 203, 207
Extraterrastrials 102-106

Fatima, Portugal 150
Fifth dimension 98
Final solution 173
Fire 90, 125-127
Floating Cradle 197, 199
Fourth Dimension 98

Garden of the Soul 162, 177, 194, 197
Genesis 69
God XIV, 4, 7, 9, 10, 12, 14, 40, 45, 49, 50, 65, 67, 68, 77, 96, 109, 113, 115, 117, 120, 124-126, 128, 129, 137, 139-144, 181, 182, 197, 201, 204, 205, 207, 212, 213
Godhead 140, 142
Good and evil 177, 178, 185, 187, 190, 212
Good Friday 111, 183
Great Spirit 144
Greek cross 100
Grof, Stanislav 63, 64, 68, 75, 83, 88, 111, 112, 116-118, 121, 122, 198, 204
Ground of the soul 115, 116
Guru 151

Hallucinations 31, 90, 164
Happy death cross 162, 163, 165, 177, 178, 205

Harvey, Andrew 151, 196
Hasidic 206
Heart piercing 117, 119
Hero's journey 13
Hidden Essence 139
Hilton, Walter 126
Hindu 68, 194, 204
Hitler energy 159, 163, 165, 176
Holocaust 163, 169, 170, 176, 205, 212
Holotropic breathwork 64-66
Holy fire 125, 127
Holy Spirit 71
Holy Trinity 113
Horizon House 29, 30
Houston, Jean 142

Ideas of reference 96, 164
Illumination 132
Intercession 153, 154, 159, 166
International Association of Near-Death Studies (IANDS) 44-46, 48, 50
Israel, Martin 128

Jewish 26, 67-69, 162, 169, 170, 174-176, 204-206, 213
Johnsen, Linda 152
Julian of Norwich 128
Jung, Carl 87, 92, 97, 188

Kaballah 67, 204, 206
Kingdom of God 212-214
Kundalini Awakening 68-72, 74, 204

Lady of Guadeloupe 166, 167
Life review 45

Magical thinking 164
Mandala 67, 113
Mark 1:10 97
Mary 150, 151, 153, 154, 165, 167,

168-170, 175, 205

Matrix Research Institute 62
Matthew 186
Menorah 212
Mental illness 10, 12, 13-15, 31, 89, 164, 208
Mohammed 205
Moody. Raymond 44
Mother Mira 151, 152, 196, 197
Muktananda 118, 141
Mysticism 20, 96, 116, 126, 130, 140, 164

Nadoloka 141
Nazis 172, 188
Near-death experience (NDE) 44-49, 204
New age 39, 213
New age thought 190

Olympia 89
Organized religion VII 4, 186, 205
Otto, Rudolf 140
Ouichel Indians 105
Out-of-body experience (OBE) 35, 38
Owl 78, 79

Panaya Kapulu 168
Pauli, Wolfgang 92
Perlman, Penny 20-23
Physics 93, 96, 164
Pope John XXIII, 168
Pope Leo XIII, 154
Power animal 78, 79
Practicum 29
Precognition 27
Progoff, Ira 130
Psychiatry VII, X, 4, 10, 13-15, 20, 28, 30, 37, 102, 165, 189, 208
Psychic abilities 39, 61
Psychology IX, 3, 10, 15, 25, 34, 93, 185, 188, 190, 204, 206

Psycho-spiritual 8, 188, 189
Psychotic 4, 14, 15, 36
Purgation 131

Reality IX, 14, 133, 144
Rebirth 57, 73, 90, 95, 114, 126, 194, 199
Reincarnation 56
Religious ideation 12, 133, 164, 211
Rinpoche, Sogyal 139, 140, 141
Rolle, Richard 126

Sacred ground of the soul 5, 116
Sahasrara 141
Saint Andrew 112
Saint Magnis 83
Saint Martin VIII
Saint Paul 154
Saint Petersburg, Russia 206
Salamander 90
Sulawesi 194
Sanskrit 68
Sarcophagus 73
Schizophrenia 12, 13, 30, 198, 208, 213
Scientific method 36
Seimer, Madeleine 127
Self 131, 132, 139, 184
Semele 89
Seven 102
Shadow 188
Shaman 64, 75, 77, 90, 195, 205
Sharp, Kimberly Clark 47
Shiva 139
Sidi Mohammed
    al-Jamal ar -Refaiss- Shadih 201
Silver ball 124
Spider 114, 124
Spirit house 160
Spiritual consciousness 38, 133
Spiritual emergency 118

Spiritual ground 12

Stigmata 110, 111, 205
Sulawesi 194
Swastika 212, 213
Swedenborg, Emmanuel 187
Synchronicity 92-96, 194, 204

Tantric 68
Tarnas, Richard 112, 113
Teresa of Avila 119
The Council of Trent 154
The Mystic Way 130, 131
Theory of Relativity 98
Three 113
Tomabalu 196
Torojaland 194, 196
Transpersonal 66, 204
Tree of life 67, 204, 206

Underhill, Evelyn 126, 127, 130
Union 133, 136, 140

Vedic 68
Vishnu 139
Viviano, Benedict V. 213, 214
Void 83, 101, 142

Walsh, Roger 86, 119, 120
Wilson, Jan 111
Whitfield, Barbara Harris 49, 50
Winged Victory 99

Yogananda 141, 142
Yom Kippur 69

Zeus 89
Ziggarat 89

About the Author

Dr. Judith Miller, a psychotherapist, traveled the globe studying world religions and cultural mythologies during her personal quest for spiritual enlightenment. She acquired insights and techniques that enabled her to expand her consciousness and achieve a new level of inner peace. Yet ironically, the inner peace she found in her personal life led her to question the fundamental principles of her profession.

She received her doctorate from Temple University and teaches at Columbia University and Beaver College. She has maintained a clinical practice since 1988 providing individual and group psychotherapy and is a consultant to public mental health facilities.

Dr. Miller conducts many workshops and her lecture presentations

include: *Advanced Theory for Healing Psychoses*, *Traveling the Mystical Path* and *Unitive Consciousness—Future of the Global Mind*. She has published in professional journals and has made numerous TV and radio appearances discussing mystical experiences, expanded consciousness and mental illness.

Dr. Miller is a member of the American Psychological Association, The American Society of Psychical Research and The Association of Transpersonal Psychology.

She currently resides in Pennsylvania with her husband Martin Miller and their dog Chewbacca.